20 YEARS OF INTERNET HUMOR

Volume Two

How the Internet Made Us Laugh, Think, and Occasionally Cringe

COMPILED BY

W.G. WILLIAMS

Published by WGWILLIAMS LLC LTD 2025

IBSN 979-8-9935622-0-9 (Paperback)
IBSN 979-8-9935622-1-6 (Digital)

Printed in the United States of America

Contents

Acknowledgements

Yes, it has been pointed out to me, frequently, that Volume One did not have any acknowledgements. Frankly, in the confusion of getting my very first book ready to be published, that was just one of MANY things that should have been included ... but weren't.

And that was probably a good thing because, until the book was in print, I had NO idea of how many people I REALLY needed to acknowledge. So, let's dive in ...

Right at the top of the list would be Jack Canfield and Steve Harrison and all their wonderful staff who put on a marvelous web-based seminar on how publishing worked. (It HAS changed tremendously over the last decade ... and continues to change at light-speed.) They taught me the first of many, many things that I needed to know, and Jack read the first draft of the book and was kind enough to provide a video interview containing a great review to get me started.

And then there is Brittany Goldsmith, my publishing coordinator at Fulton Books. Brittany has put up with a year of my calls, e-mails, and musing about what was going on, what was taking so long, why was this or that happening, and why does THAT have to be THIS way. She never lost her temper and always was able to come up with an answer that calmed me down.

Once the book was out, Cristina Smith, Steve's publishing and marketing trainer, was able to provide weekly sessions on marketing techniques that proved invaluable.

And of course, there are my wife Jean and daughters Carrie and Erin who have spent the last 30 years (most of the girls' lives) with me sending daily emails and never really understanding what I was doing or why. And now that the first volume is out, I'm spending even more time at the computer and doing podcasts and marketing. Truly, these three deserve the greatest acknowledgement possible for putting up with me ... and continuing to do so because there are more volumes coming out!

And finally, thanks to several dozen friends on my Launch Team who provided moral support as the launch day approached and then bought an introductory eBook from Amazon to get the sales started.

And I'm sure there are many others who will occur to me as soon as I submit this for publication. Watch for them in the next volume.

Introduction

Back Into the Abyss

When I put together the first volume of *20 Years of Internet Humor*, I imagined it as a sort of digital time capsule — a record of the bizarre, brilliant, and occasionally baffling ways we've made each other laugh online. I figured I'd said what I needed to say to get things started since there's still a lot more to be added!

Turns out: REALLY a lot more...and this is the next step!

Not because the internet changed — though it does continuously — but because people didn't stop being funny. Not for a minute. They kept making things: absurd things, clever things, things so stupid they looped all the way back around to genius. And I kept collecting. Not on purpose, at first. Just a saved image here, a snippet of text there, a half-remembered in-joke from a long-deleted page. Before long, I realized I hadn't closed the door behind me — I'd just walked into another room.

This second volume is the result of that slow accumulation, a sequel born not from obligation but compulsion. Because once you've spent enough time in the trenches of internet humor — forums, imageboards, forgotten websites with page counters still proudly ticking — you start to feel a strange responsibility. Someone ought to remember the nonsense. Someone should make sure the chain emails, the surreal flash animations, the ASCII absurdities and cryptic in-jokes don't fade into digital oblivion.

So here we are again.

This isn't a greatest-hits album. Some of what's in here is obscure by design. Some of them are uncomfortably close to the bone. Some entries don't even make sense anymore — if they ever did. But all of it, in some way, reflects the joy of creating something funny for no reason other than to make someone, somewhere, laugh...or think!

That's the beauty of it, really. No likes. No followers. Just humor and human interest in their purest, weirdest forms — made by people, shared with people, and kept alive by nothing more than memory and a stubborn refusal to let the punchline die.

So once again, welcome. Take your time, lose track of it, and enjoy this second plunge into the chaos.

I promise: it's still very worth it.

— Bill Williams

A Rant from the Over-30 Crowd...

When I was a kid, adults used to bore me to tears with
their tedious diatribes about how hard things were when
they were growing up; what with walking twenty-five miles
to school every morning ... Uphill BOTH ways

Yadda, yadda, yadda

And I remember promising myself that when I grew up, there
was no way I was going to lay a bunch of crap like that on
kids about how hard I had it and how easy they've got it!
But now that I'm over the ripe old age of thirty, I can't help but
look around and notice the youth of today. You've got it so easy!
I mean, compared to my childhood, you live in a damn Utopia!
And I hate to say it, but you kids today don't
know how good you've got it!
I mean, when I was a kid, we didn't have The Internet. If
we wanted to know something, we had to go to the damn
library and look it up ourselves in the card catalog!
There was no email! We had to actually write
somebody a letter…with a pen!
Then you had to walk all the way across the street and put it
in the mailbox, and it would take like a week to get there!

There were no MP3's or Napster's! If you wanted to steal music,
you had to hitchhike to the record store and shoplift it yourself!
Or you had to wait around all day to tape it off the radio and
the DJ'd usually talk over the beginning and mess it all up!

We didn't have fancy crap like Call Waiting! If you were on the phone and somebody else called, they got a busy signal, that's it!

And we didn't have fancy Caller ID Boxes either!
When the phone rang, you had no idea who it was! It could
be your school, your mom, your boss, your bookie, your
drug dealer, a collections agent. You just didn't know!!!
You had to pick it up and take your chances, mister!

We didn't have any fancy Sony PlayStation video games with high-resolution 3-D graphics! We had the Atari 2600 with games like
"Space Invaders" and "Asteroids." Your guy was a little square!
You actually had to use your imagination! And there were no
multiple levels or screens, it was just one screen forever and
you could never win. The game just kept getting harder and
harder and faster and faster until you died! Just like LIFE!

When you went to the movie theater there no such thing as stadium
seating! All the seats were the same height! If a tall guy or some old broad
with a hat sat in front of you and you couldn't see, you were just screwed!

Sure, we had cable television, but back then that was only like 15
channels and there was no on-screen menu and no remote! You had
to use a little book called a TV Guide to find out what was on!
You were screwed when it came to channel surfing! You
had to get off your butt and walk over to the TV to change
the channel. And there was no Cartoon Network either!
You could only get cartoons on Saturday Morning.
Do you hear what I'm saying!?!
We had to wait ALL WEEK for cartoons!

And we didn't have microwaves. If we wanted to heat something
up we had to use the stove or go build a frigging fire …
Imagine that!
If we wanted popcorn, we had to use that stupid Jiffy Pop
thin and shake it over the stove forever like an idiot.

That's exactly what I'm talking about! You kids today have got it too easy. You're spoiled. You guys wouldn't have lasted five minutes back in 1980!

Regards,
The over 30 Crowd

Contributed by David A. Silverman
11/10/2008

A Senior Moment ... at 48?

By David McClure
Dallas Morning News
Sunday, June 28, 2009

$5.37. That's what the kid behind the counter at Taco Bueno said to me. I dug into my pocket and pulled out some lint and two dimes and something that used to be a Jolly Rancher. Having already handed the kid a five-spot, I started to head back out to the truck to grab some change when the kid with the Elmo hairdo said the harshest thing anyone has ever said to me. He said, "It's OK. I'll just give you the senior citizen discount."

I turned to see who he was talking to and then heard the sound of change hitting the counter in front of me. "Only $4.68" he said cheerfully. I stood there stupefied. I am 48, not even 50 yet a mere child! Senior citizen?

I took my burrito and walked out to the truck wondering what was wrong with Elmo. Was he blind? As I sat in the truck, my blood began to boil. Old? Me?

I'll show him, I thought. I opened the door and headed back inside. I strode to the counter, and there he was waiting with a smile.

Before I could say a word, he held up something and jingled it in front of me, like I could be that easily distracted! What am I now? A toddler?

"Dude! Can't get too far without your car keys, eh?"

I stared with utter disdain at the keys. I began to rationalize in my mind. "Leaving keys behind hardly makes a man elderly! It could happen to anyone!"

I turned and headed back to the truck. I slipped the key into the ignition, but it wouldn't turn. What now? I checked my keys and tried another. Still nothing. That's when I noticed the purple beads hanging from my rearview mirror. I had no purple beads hanging from my rearview mirror.

Then, a few other objects came into focus. The car seat in the back seat. Happy Meal toys spread all over the floorboard. A partially eaten doughnut on the dashboard.

Faster than you can say ginkgo biloba, I flew out of the alien vehicle. Moments later I was speeding out of the parking lot, relieved to finally be leaving this nightmarish stop in my life. That is when I felt it, deep in the bowels of my stomach: hunger! My stomach growled and churned, and I reached to grab my burrito, only it was nowhere to be found.

I swung the truck around, gathered my courage, and strode back into the restaurant one final time. There Elmo stood, draped in youth and black nail polish. All I could think was, "What is the world coming to?" All I could say was, "Did I leave my food and drink in here?" At this point I was ready to ask a Boy Scout to help me back to my vehicle and then go straight home and apply for Social Security benefits.

Elmo had no clue. I walked back out to the truck, and suddenly a young lad came up and tugged on my jeans to get my attention. He was holding up a drink and a bag. His mother explained, "I think you left this in my truck by mistake." I took the food and drink from the little boy and sheepishly apologized.

She offered these kind words: "It's OK. My grandfather does stuff like this all the time."

All of this is to explain how I got a ticket doing 85 in a 40. Yes, I was racing some punk kid in a Toyota Prius. And "No," I told the officer, "I'm not too old to be driving this fast."

As I walked in the front door, my wife met me halfway down the hall. I handed her a bag of cold food and a $300 speeding ticket. I promptly sat in my rocking chair and covered up my legs with a blanky.

The good news was I had successfully found my way home.

Printed with permission of David McClure who teaches science and coaches at Faubion Middle School in McKinney, Texas. He is also a "Teacher Voices" volunteer columnist. His email address is dmcclure9066@yahoo.com.

Contributed by Kay Reynolds
8/10/2009

A Swiss Hanukkah

A Short Play by David Lipschutz

Lights up on AVI, a Jewish man, aged 35-45.
He is sitting on his grandmother's sofa, complete
with flower print, doilies, and plastic covering.

AVI: What does Hanukkah mean to me?
(laughs to self) Believe it or not, it means
"The Alps." Not because I've been there, oh g-d no.

You see, my Bubbie and Zayde, of blessed memory, loved the Alps.
In fact, they loved it so much, their basement was professionally done up
to look like you were standing on a terrace
overlooking the mountains. I'm not kidding.
They literally painted the walls and put up
these wood planks and railings.
As my Bubbie would say, "It's the Swiss Alps in
fresco complimenting the Swiss chalet."
Not exactly sure what any of those words mean, but…
Yup, I can definitely see it.

(beat)

We, um, we always opened our presents in their basement.
So, for eight days a year, my Hanukkah consisted of traveling
from this ranch-style house in the suburbs of Chicago to this
beautiful Alpine Chateau in Europe just by going downstairs.
Some really hopeful memories there.
I miss that fake skyline almost as much as I miss my Bubbie and Zayde.
(beat)
Now, let me tell you about their *lladro* collection…

Lights slowly fade until blackout.

Contributed by David Lipschutz
12/9/2023

An Honest Lawyer...

An investment counselor went out on her own. She was shrewd and diligent, so business kept coming in. Pretty soon she realized she needed an in-house counsel, and so she began interviewing young lawyers.

"As I'm sure you can understand," she started off with one of the first applicants, "in a business like this, our personal integrity must be beyond question." She leaned forward. "Mr. Peterson, are you an 'honest' lawyer?"

"Honest?" replied the job prospect. "Let me tell you something about honesty. Why, I'm so honest that my father lent me fifteen thousand dollars for my education, and I paid back every penny the minute I tried my very first case."

"Impressive. And what sort of case was that?"

The lawyer squirmed in his seat and admitted,
"He sued me for the money."

Contributed by David Taylor
4/11/2006

Ten Best Caddie Responses

Number: 10
Golfer: "I think I 'm going to drown myself in the lake."
Caddy: "Think you can keep your head down that long, sir?"

Number: 9
Golfer: "I 'd move heaven and earth to break 100 on this course."
Caddy: "Try heaven sir, you 've already moved most of the earth."

Number: 8
Golfer: "Do you think my game is improving?"
Caddy: "Yes sir … You miss the ball much closer now."

Number: 7
Golfer: "Do you think I can get there with a 5 iron?"
Caddy: "Eventually, sir."

Number: 6
Golfer: "You've got to be the worst caddy in the world."
Caddy: "I don 't think so sir . . . That would
be too much of a coincidence."

Number: 5
Golfer: "Please stop checking your watch all the
time. It's too much of a distraction."
Caddy: "It's not a watch sir - it's a compass."

Number: 4
Golfer: "How do you like my game?"
Caddy: "It's very good sir - but personally, I prefer golf."

Number: 3
Golfer: "Do you think it's a sin to play on Sunday?
Caddy: "I 'm afraid the way you play sir, it's a sin on any day."

Number: 2
Golfer: "This is the worst course I 've ever played on."
Caddy: "But this isn't the golf course . . .. We left that an hour ago sir."

And the Number: 1 ... Best Caddy Comment:

Golfer: "That can 't be my ball, it's too old."
Caddy: "It's been a long time since we teed off, sir."

Bonus ...

An old favorite ... about the Golfer who has been
slicing off the tee at every hole . . ..
He finally gives up and asks his long-suffering caddy ...
Golfer: "Can you see any obvious problems?"
Caddy: "There's a piece of **** on the end of your club."
The Golfer picks up his club and cleans the club face ...
Caddy: "No sir, it's at the other end."

**Contributed by Judy Flahiff
4/10/2019**

Calling In Sick...

Calling in sick to work makes me uncomfortable. No matter how legitimate my excuse is, I always get the feeling that my boss thinks I'm lying.

On one recent occasion, I had a valid reason but lied anyway because the truth was just too darned humiliating. I simply mentioned that I had sustained a head injury, and I hoped I would feel up to coming in the next day. By then, I reasoned, I could think up a doozy to explain the bandage on the top of my head.

The accident occurred mainly because I had given in to my wife's wishes to adopt a cute little kitty.

Initially, the new acquisition was no problem. Then one morning, I was taking my shower after breakfast when I heard my wife, Deb, call out to me from the kitchen.

"Honey! The garbage disposal is dead again. Please come reset it."

"You know where the button is," I protested through the shower pitter-patter and steam. "Reset it yourself!"

"But I'm scared!" she persisted. "What if it starts going and sucks me in?" There was a meaningful pause and then, "C'mon, it'll only take you a second."

So out I came, dripping wet and butt naked, hoping that my silent outraged nudity would make a statement about how I perceived her behavior as extremely cowardly.

Sighing loudly, I squatted down and stuck my head under the sink to find the button. That was the last action I remember performing.

It struck without warning and without any respect to my circumstances. No, it wasn't the hexed disposal, drawing me into its gnashing metal teeth. It was our new kitty who discovered the fascinating dangling objects she spied hanging between my legs. She had been poised around the corner and stalked me as I reached under the sink. And, at the precise moment when I was most vulnerable, she leapt at the toys I unwittingly offered and snagged them with her needle-like claws.

I lost all rational thought to control orderly bodily movements, blindly rising at a violent rate of speed, with the full weight of a kitten hanging from my masculine region.

Wild animals are sometimes faced with a "fight or flight" syndrome. Men, in this predicament, choose only the "flight" option. I know this from experience. I was fleeing straight up into the air when the sink and cabinet bluntly and forcefully impeded my ascent. The impact knocked me out cold.

When I awoke, my wife and the paramedics stood over me. Now there are not many things in this life worse than finding oneself lying on the kitchen floor butt naked in front of a group of "been-there, done-that" paramedics.

Even worse, having been fully briefed by my wife, the paramedics were all snorting loudly as they tried to conduct their work, all the while trying to suppress their hysterical laughter ... and not succeeding.

Somehow, I lived through it all. A few days later I finally made it back into the office, where colleagues tried to coax an explanation out of me about my head injury. I kept silent, claiming it was too painful to talk about ... which it was.

"What's the matter?" They all asked, "Cat got your tongue?"

If they only knew!

Contributed by David Taylor
4/28/2006

Christmas Cookie Rules...

1. If you eat a Christmas cookie fresh out of the oven, it has no calories because everyone knows that the first cookie is the test and thus calorie free.

2. If you drink a diet soda after eating your second cookie, it also has no calories because the diet soda cancels out the cookie calories.

3. If a friend comes over while you're making your Christmas cookies and needs to sample, you must sample with your friend. Because your friend's first cookie is calories free, rule #1 is yours also. It would be rude to let your friend sample alone and, being the friend that you are, that makes your cookie calorie free.

4. Any cookie calories consumed while walking around will fall to your feet and eventually fall off as you move. This is due to gravity and the density of the caloric mass.

5. Any calories consumed during the frosting of the Christmas cookies will be used up because it takes many calories to lick excess frosting from a knife without cutting your tongue.

6. Cookies colored red or green have very few calories. Red ones have three and green ones have five - one calorie for each letter. Make more red ones!

7. Cookies eaten while watching "Miracle on 34th Street" have no calories because they are part of the entertainment package and not part of one's personal fuel.

8. As always, cookie pieces contain no calories because the process of breaking causes calorie leakage.

9. Any cookies consumed from someone else's plate have no calories since the calories rightfully belong to the other person and will cling to their plate. We all know how calories like to CLING!

10. Any cookies consumed while feeling stressed have no calories because cookies used for medicinal purposes NEVER have calories. It's a rule!

Contributed by Bubba & Bonnie Mehling
12/2/2008

Don't Bring Plants Indoors...

Garden Grass Snakes (also known as Garter Snakes) can be dangerous. Yes, grass snakes, not rattlesnakes. Here's why.

A couple in Sweetwater, Texas, had a lot of potted plants. During a recent cold spell, the wife was bringing a lot of them indoors to protect them from a possible freeze.

It turned out that a little green garden grass snake was hidden in one of the plants and when it had warmed up, it slithered out and the wife saw it go under the sofa. She let out a very loud scream. The husband (who was taking a shower) ran out into the living room naked to see what the problem was.

She told him there was a snake under the sofa. He got down on the floor on his hands and knees to look for it. About that time, the family dog came and cold-nosed him on the behind. He thought the snake had bitten him, so he screamed and fell over on the floor.

His wife thought he had a heart attack, so she covered him up, told him to lie still, and called an ambulance. The attendants rushed in, wouldn't listen to his protests, loaded him on the stretcher, and started carrying him out

About that time, the snake came out from under the sofa and the Emergency Medical Technician saw it and dropped his end of the stretcher. That's when the man broke his leg and why he is still in the hospital.

The wife still had the problem of the snake in the house, so she called on a neighbor man. He volunteered to capture the snake. He armed himself with a rolled-up newspaper and began poking under the couch. Soon he decided it was gone and told the woman, who sat down on the sofa in relief.

But while relaxing, her hand dangled in between the cushions where she felt the snake wriggling around. She screamed and fainted, and the snake rushed back under the sofa.

The neighbor, seeing her lying there passed out, tried to use CPR to revive her. The neighbor's wife, who had just returned from shopping at the grocery store, saw her husband's mouth on the woman's mouth and slammed her husband in the back of the head with a bag of canned goods, knocking him out and cutting his scalp to a point where it needed stitches.

The noise woke the woman from her dead faint, and she saw her neighbor lying on the floor with his wife bending over him. She assumed he had been bitten by the snake; she went to the kitchen and got a bottle of whiskey and began pouring it down the man's throat.

By now the police had arrived. They saw the unconscious man, smelled the whiskey and assumed that a drunken fight had occurred. They were about to arrest them all when the women tried to explain how it all happened over a little green snake.

The police called an ambulance which took away the neighbor and his sobbing wife. The little snake again crawled out from under the sofa. One of the policemen drew his gun and fired at it. He missed the snake and hit the leg of the end table. The table fell over and the lamp on it shattered and, as the bulb broke, it started a fire in the drapes.

The second policeman tried to beat out the flames and fell through the window into the yard on top of the family dog who, startled, jumped out and raced into the street where an oncoming car swerved to avoid it and smashed into the parked police car.

Meanwhile, the burning drapes were seen by the neighbors who called the fire department. The firemen had started raising the fire truck ladder when they were halfway down the street. The rising ladder tore out the overhead wires and put out the electricity and disconnected the telephones in a ten-square city block area (but they did get the house fire out).

Time passed. Both men were discharged from the hospital; the house was repaired; the dog came home; the police acquired a new car; and all was right with their world.

A while later they were watching TV, and the weatherman announced a cold snap for that night. The husband asked his wife if she thought they should bring in their plants for the night.

That's when she shot him.

Contributed by Susan Luna
2/10/2006

Driving in Dallas

For all my friends and family that have never ventured to Dallas, Daalis, or Dallus, here is an aerial view of a highways intersection that is fairly close to where we live.

First you must learn to pronounce the city's name. It is DAL-LUS, or DAA-LIS depending on if you live inside or outside LBJ Freeway.

Next, if your Mapsco is more than a few weeks old, throw it out and buy a new one. If in Denton County and your Mapsco is one day old, then it is already obsolete. Forget the traffic rules you learned elsewhere. (Frisco has screwed everything up.)

Dallas has its own version of traffic rules... "Hold on and pray." There is no such thing as a dangerous high-speed chase in Dallas. We all drive like that.

All directions start with, "Get on Beltline," which has no beginning and no end. (It REALLY DOESN'T!!!)

The morning rush hour is from 6 to 10. The evening rush hour is from 3 to 7. Friday's rush hour starts Thursday morning.

If you actually stop at a yellow light, you will be rear-ended, cussed out and possibly shot. When you are the first one on the starting line, count to five when the light turns green before going to avoid crashing with all the drivers running the red light in cross-traffic.

Construction on Central Expressway is a way of life and a permanent form of entertainment. We had sooo much fun with that, we have added George Bush Freeway and the High Five to the mix.

All unexplained sights are explained by the phrase, "Oh, we're in Fort Worth!"

If someone actually has his or her turn signal on, it is probably a factory defect. Car horns are actually "Road Rage" indicators - and remember, it's legal to be armed in Texas.

All old ladies with blue hair in a Mercedes have the right of way. Period. And remember, it's legal to be armed in Texas.

Inwood Road, Plano Road, NW Highway, East Grand, Garland Road, Marsh Lane, Josey Lane, 15th Street, Preston Road all mysteriously change names as you cross intersections (these are only a FEW examples). The perfect example is what is MOSTLY known as Plano Road. On the south end, it is known as Lake Highlands Drive, cross Northwest Highway and it becomes Plano Road, go about 8 miles and it is briefly Greenville Ave, Ave K, and Highway 5. It ends in Sherman.

The North Dallas Tollway is our daily version of NASCAR. The minimum acceptable speed on the Dallas North Toll Road is 85 mph. Anything less is considered downright sissy. It also ends in Sherman.

If asking directions in Irving or SE Dallas, you must have knowledge of Spanish. If in central Richardson or on Harry Hines, Mandarin Chinese will be your best bet. If you stop to ask directions on Gaston or Live Oak, you better be armed... and remember, it's legal to be armed in Texas. The wrought iron on windows near Oak Cliff and Fair Park is not ornamental!

A trip across town east to west will take a minimum of four hours, although many north/south freeways have unposted minimum speeds of 75. It is possible to be driving WEST in the NORTH-bound lane of EAST NORTHWEST Highway. Don't let this confuse you.

LBJ is called "The Death Trap" for two reasons: "death" and "trap."

If it's 100 degrees, Thanksgiving must be next weekend. If it's 10 degrees and sleeting/snowing, the Fort Worth Stock Show is going on. If it has rained 6 inches in the last hour, the Byron Nelson Golf Classic is in the second round (if it's Spring) - and it is the Texas State Fair if it's Fall. If you go to the Fair, pay the $15.00 to park INSIDE Fair Park. Parking elsewhere could cost up to $2500 for damages, towing fees, parking tickets, and possibly a gunshot wound. If some guy with a flag tries to get you to park in his yard, run over him.

Any amusement parks, stadiums, arenas, racetracks, airports, etc., are conveniently located as far away from EVERYTHING as possible to allow for ample parking on grassy areas.

Final Warning: Don't Mess with Texas Drivers ... remember, it's legal to Be armed in Texas.

Contributed by Eldon Reynolds
4/18/2024

The Flat Tarr...

There was this fellow from "down south" who had a flat tire.
He pulled off on the side of the road, jumped out of his car,
walked down the hillside and picked a bunch of wildflowers.
He proceeded to put one bouquet of flowers in front of the car
and one behind it. Then he got back in the car to wait.

A passerby studied the scene as he drove by and was so curious, he turned
around and went back. He asked the fellow what the problem was.

The man replied, "I have a flat tarr."

In response the passerby asked, "But what's with the flowers?"

The man responded, "When you break down, they tell you to put flares
in the front and flares in the back! I never did understand it neither."

Contributed by Bubba and Bonnie Mehling
8/15/2005

Fun Facts

1. "Paper" money isn't made out of paper, it's made out of cotton.

2. The Declaration of Independence was written on hemp (marijuana) paper.

3. The dot over the letter i is called a "tittle."

4. A raisin dropped in a glass of fresh champagne will bounce up and down continuously from the bottom of the glass to the top.

5. Susan Lucci is the daughter of Phyllis Diller.

6. 40% of Mc Donald's profits come from the sales of Happy Meals.

7. 315 entries in Webster's 1996 Dictionary were misspelled.

8. The "spot" on 7UP comes from its inventor, who had red eyes. He was albino.

9. On average, 12 newborns will be given to the wrong parents daily.

10. Warren Beatty and Shirley MacLaine are brother and sister.

11. Chocolate affects a dog's heart and nervous system; a few ounces will kill a small-sized dog.

12. Orcas (killer whales) kill sharks by torpedoing up into the shark's stomach from underneath.

13. Most lipstick contains fish scales.

14. Donald Duck comics were banned from Finland because he doesn't wear pants.

15. Ketchup was sold in the 1830's as medicine.

16. Upper and lower-case letters are named "upper" and "lower" because in the time when all original print had to be set in individual letters, the "upper case" letters were stored in the case on top of the case that stored the smaller, "lower case" letters.

17. Leonardo Da Vinci could write with one hand and draw with the other at the same time, hence, multi-tasking was invented.

18. Because metal was scarce, the Oscars given out during World War II were made of wood.

19. There are no clocks in Las Vegas gambling casinos.

20. The name Wendy was made up for the book Peter Pan; there was never a recorded Wendy before!

21. There are no words in the dictionary that rhyme with: orange, purple, or silver!

22. Leonardo DaVinci invented scissors. Also, it took him 10 years to paint Mona Lisa's lips.

23. A tiny amount of liquor on a scorpion will make it instantly go mad and sting itself to death.

24. The mask used by Michael Myers in the original "Halloween" was a Captain Kirk mask painted white.

25. If you have three quarters, four dimes, and four pennies, you have $1.19. You also have the largest amount of money in coins without being able to make change for a dollar.

26. By raising your legs slowly and lying on your back, you can't sink in quicksand.

27. The phrase "rule of thumb" is derived from an old English law, which stated that you couldn't beat your wife with anything wider than your thumb.

28. The first product Motorola started to develop was a record player for automobiles. At that time, the most known player on the market was the Victrola, so they called themselves Motorola.

29. Celery has negative calories! It takes more calories to eat a piece of celery than the celery has in it to begin with. It's the same with apples.

30. Chewing gum while peeling onions will keep you from crying!

31. The glue on Israeli postage stamps is certified kosher.

32. "Guinness Book of Records" holds the record for being the book most often stolen from public Libraries.

33. Astronauts are not allowed to eat beans before they go into space because passing wind in a space suit damages it.

34. George Carlin said it best about Martha Stewart. "Boy, I feel a lot safer now that she's behind bars. O.J. Simpson and Kobe Bryant are still walking around; Osama Bin Laden too, but they take the ONE woman in America willing to cook, clean, and work in the yard, and they haul her off to jail."

Contributed by Bubba & Bonnie Mehling
06/02/2010

Gardening Made Easy...

An old Italian American lived alone in New Jersey. He wanted to plant his annual tomato garden, but it was very difficult work as the ground was hard. His only son, Vincent, who used to help him, was in prison. The old man wrote a letter to his son and described his predicament:

Dear Vincent,

I am feeling pretty sad because it looks like I won't be able to plant my tomato garden this year. I'm just getting too old to be digging up a garden plot. I know if you were here my troubles would be over. I know you would be happy to dig the plot for me, like in the old days.

Love, Papa

A few days later he received a letter from his son.

Dear Pop,

Don't dig up that garden. That's where the bodies are buried.

Love, Vinnie

Early the next morning, FBI agents and local police arrived and dug up the entire area without finding any bodies. They apologized to the old man and left.

The next day the old man received another letter from his son.

Dear Pop,

Go ahead and plant the tomatoes now. That's the best I could do under the circumstances.

Love you, Vinnie

Contributed by Julius Graw
5/21/2009

God's Cake

Sometimes we wonder, "What did I do to deserve this?" or "Why did God have to do this to me?" Here is a wonderful explanation: A daughter is telling her mother how everything is going wrong, she's failing algebra, her boyfriend broke up with her and her best friend is moving away.

Meanwhile, her mother is baking a cake and asks her daughter if she would like a snack, and the daughter says, "Absolutely Mom, I love your cake."

"Here, have some cooking oil," her mother offers.
"Yuck!" says her daughter.
"How about a couple of raw eggs?"
"Gross, Mom!"
"Would you like some flour then? Or maybe baking soda?"
"Mom, those are all yucky!"

To which the mother replies: "Yes, all those things seem bad all by themselves. But when they are put together in the right way, they make a wonderfully delicious cake!"

God works the same way. Many times we wonder why He would let us go through such difficult times. But God knows that when He puts these things all in His order, they always work for good! We just have to trust Him and, eventually, they will all make something wonderful!

Contributed by Ron Heisler
12/16/2008

Government and Politics in Action...

DEMOCRATIC CONTROL
* You have two cows.
* Your neighbor has none.
* You feel guilty for being successful.

REPUBLICAN CONTROL
* You have two cows.
* Your neighbor has none.
* So?

SOCIALIST CONTROL
* You have two cows.
* The government takes one and gives it to your neighbor.
* You form a cooperative to tell him how to manage his cow.

COMMUNIST CONTROL
* You have two cows.
* The government seizes both and provides you with milk.
* You wait in line for hours to get it.
* It is expensive and sour.

CAPITALISM - AMERICAN STYLE
* You have two cows.
* You sell one, buy a bull, and build a herd of cows.

BUREAUCRACY - AMERICAN STYLE
* You have two cows.
* Under the new farm program the government pays you to shoot one, milk the other, and then pour the milk down the drain.

AMERICAN CORPORATION
* You have two cows.
* You sell one, lease it back to yourself and do an IPO on the 2nd one.
* You force the two cows to produce the milk of four cows. You are surprised when one cow drops dead. You spin an announcement to the analysts stating you have downsized and are reducing expenses.
* Your stock goes up.

FRENCH CORPORATION
* You have two cows.
* You go on strike because you want three cows.
* You go to lunch and drink wine.
* Life is good.

JAPANESE CORPORATION
* You have two cows.
* You redesign them so they are one-tenth the size of an ordinary cow and produce twenty times the milk.
* They learn to travel on unbelievably crowded trains.
* Most are at the top of their class at cow school.

GERMAN CORPORATION
* You have two cows.
* You engineer them so they are all blond, drink lots of beer, give excellent quality milk, and run a hundred miles an hour.
* Unfortunately they also demand 13 weeks of vacation per year.

ITALIAN CORPORATION
* You have two cows but you don't know where they are.
* While ambling around, you see a beautiful woman.
* You break for lunch.
* Life is good.

RUSSIAN CORPORATION

* You have two cows.
* You have some vodka.
* You count them and learn you have five cows.
* You have some more vodka.
* You count them again and learn you have 42 cows.
* the Mafia shows up and takes over however many cows you really have.

TALIBAN CORPORATION

* You have all the cows in Afghanistan, which are two.
* You don't milk them because you cannot touch any creature's private parts.
* You get a $40 million grant from the US government to find alternatives to milk production but use the money to buy weapons.

IRAQI CORPORATION

* You have two cows.
* They go into hiding.
* They send radio tapes of their mooing.

POLISH CORPORATION

* You have two bulls.
* Employees are regularly maimed and killed attempting to milk them.

BELGIAN CORPORATION

* You have one cow.
* The cow is schizophrenic.
* Sometimes the cow thinks he's French, other times he's Flemish.
* The Flemish cow won't share with the French cow.
* The French cow wants control of the Flemish cow's milk.
* The cow asks permission to be cut in half.
* The cow dies happy.

FLORIDA CORPORATION
* You have a black cow and a brown cow.
* Everyone votes for the best looking one.
* Some of the people who actually like the brown one best acciden-tally vote for the black one.
* Some people vote for both.
* Some people vote for neither.
* Some people can't figure out how to vote at all.
* Finally, a bunch of guys from out-of-state tell you which one you think is the best-looking cow.

CALIFORNIA CORPORATION
* You have millions of cows.
* They make real California cheese.
* Only five speak English.
* Most are illegal.
* Arnold likes the ones with the big udders.

Contributed by David A. Silverman
12/29/2005

Here's a New Way of Looking at an Old Equation...

1 To find a woman you need Time and Money therefore:

$$\text{Woman} = \text{Time} \times \text{Money}$$

2 "Time is money" so

$$\text{Time} = \text{Money}$$

3 Therefore

$$\text{Woman} = \text{Money} \times \text{Money}$$

$$\text{Woman} = (\text{Money})^2$$

4 "Money is the root of all problems"

$$\text{Money} = \sqrt{\text{Problems}}$$

5 Therefore

$$\text{Woman} = (\sqrt{\text{Problems}})^2$$

$$\text{Woman} = \text{Problems}$$

A^+

Contributed by Gary Thornton
10/13/2005

I Want a Priest!

A Catholic man was struck by a bus on a busy street. He was lying near death on the sidewalk as a crowd gathered. "A priest. Somebody get me a priest!" the man gasped.

Minutes dragged on and no one stepped out of the crowd. A policeman checked the crowd and finally yelled, "A PRIEST, PLEASE! Isn't there a priest in this crowd to give this man his last rites?"

Finally, out of the crowd stepped a little old Jewish man of at least 80 years of age.

"Mr. Policeman," he said. "I'm not a priest. I'm not even a Christian. But for 50 years now I'm living behind the Catholic Church on First Avenue, and every night I'm overhearing their services. I can recall a lot of it, and maybe I can be of some comfort to this poor man."

The policeman agreed and cleared the crowd so the man could get through to where the injured man lay.

The old Jewish man knelt down, leaned over the prostrate man and said in a solemn voice:

"B-4 --- I-19 --- N-38 --- G-54 --- O-72"

Contributed by Susan Luna
10/04/2005

Investing in Your Retirement

If you had purchased $1000.00 of Nortel stock five years ago, it would now be worth $49.00.

With Enron, you would have had $16.50 left of the original $1,000.00.

With WorldCom, you would have had less than $5.00 left.

But, if you had purchased $1,000.00 worth of beer, drank all the beer, then turned in the cans for the aluminum recycling REFUND, you would have had $214.00.

Based on the above, current investment advice is to drink heavily and recycle.

It's called the 401-Keg Plan

Contributed by Ron Gargasz
4/6/2006

"Is It Better to Be a Jock or A Nerd?"

Michael Jordan made over $300,000 a game. That equals $10,000 a minute at an average of 30 minutes of playing time per game. With $40 million in endorsements, he made $178,100 a day, working or not.

* If he sleeps seven hours a night, he makes $52,000 every night while visions of sugarplums dance in his head.
* If he goes to see a movie, it'll cost him $9.50, but he'll make $18,550 while he's there.
* If he decides to have a five minute egg, he'll make $618 while boiling it.
* He makes $7,415/hour more than minimum wage.
* He'd make $3,710 while watching each episode of Friends.
* If he wanted to save up for a new Acura SLX (about $90,000) it would take him a whole 12 hours.
* If someone were to hand him his salary and endorsement money, they would have to do it at the rate of $2.00 every second.
* He'd probably pay around $200 for a nice round of golf, but will be reimbursed around $30,000 during that round.
* Assuming he puts the federal maximum into a tax deferred account (401k), he will hit the federal cap at 8:30 a.m. on January 1st.
* If you were given a penny for every 10 dollars he made, you'd be living comfortably at $65,000 a year.
* He'd make about $19.60 while watching the 100 meter dash in the Olympics.
* He'd make about $15,600 during the Boston Marathon.
* While the common person is spending about $20 for a meal in his trendy Chicago restaurant, he'd pull in about $5,600.

*   In his last year, he made more than twice as much as all U.S. past presidents for all of their terms combined.

However...

If Jordan saves 100% of his income for the next 250 years, he'll still have less than Bill Gates has today.

Game over. Nerd wins.

Contributed by David Taylor
3/12/2007

Kids' Thoughts on Marriage...

HOW DO YOU DECIDE WHO TO MARRY?

*You got to find somebody who likes the same stuff. Like, if
you like sports, she should like it that you like sports, and
she should keep the chips and dip and beer coming.*
-- Alan, age 10

*No person really decides before they grow up who they're going to marry. God
decides it all way before, and you get to find out later who you're stuck with.*
-- Kristen, age 10

WHAT IS THE RIGHT AGE TO GET MARRIED?

Twenty-three is the best age because you know the person FOREVER by then.
-- Camille, age 10

HOW CAN A STRANGER TELL IF TWO
PEOPLE ARE MARRIED?

*You might have to guess, based on whether they
seem to be yelling at the same kids.*
-- Derrick, age 8

WHAT DO YOU THINK YOUR MOM
AND DAD HAVE IN COMMON?

Both don't want any more kids.
-- Lori, age 8

WHAT DO MOST PEOPLE DO ON A DATE?

*Dates are for having fun, and people should use them to get to know
each other. Even boys have something to say if you listen long enough.*
-- Lynnette, age 8

On the first date, they just tell each other lies and that usually gets them interested enough to go for a second date.
-- Martin, age 10

WHAT WOULD YOU DO ON A FIRST DATE THAT WAS TURNING SOUR?

I'd run home and play dead. The next day I would call all the newspapers and make sure they wrote about me in all the dead columns.
-- Craig, age 9

WHEN IS IT OKAY TO KISS SOMEONE?

When they're rich.
-- Pam, age 7

The law says you have to be eighteen, so I wouldn't want to mess with that.
- - Curt, age 7

The rule goes like this: If you kiss someone, then you should marry them and have kids with them. It's the right thing to do.
-- Howard, age 8

IS IT BETTER TO BE SINGLE OR MARRIED?

It's better for girls to be single but not for boys. Boys need someone to clean up after them.
-- Anita, age 9

HOW WOULD THE WORLD BE DIFFERENT IF PEOPLE DIDN'T GET MARRIED?

There sure would be a lot of kids to explain, wouldn't there?
-- Kelvin, age 8

HOW WOULD YOU MAKE A MARRIAGE WORK?

Tell your wife that she looks pretty, even if she looks like a truck.
-- Ricky, age 10

Contributed by E.W. Hallford
5/11/2009

Lord's Prayer

The Lord's Prayer is not allowed in many U.S. Public schools today so a 15-year-old student in Minnesota wrote the following NEW School Prayer (and got an A+)

Now I sit me down in school,
Where praying is against the rule.
For this great nation under God
Finds mention of Him very odd.

If scripture now the class recites,
It violates the Bill of Rights.
And anytime my head I bow,
Becomes a Federal matter now.

Our hair can be purple, orange or green,
That's no offense; it's a freedom scene.
The law is specific, the law is precise.
Prayers spoken aloud are a serious vice.

For praying in a public hall
Might offend someone with no faith at all.
In silence alone we must meditate,
God's name is prohibited by the State.

We're allowed to cuss and dress like freaks,
And pierce our noses, tongues, and cheeks.
They've outlawed guns, but FIRST the Bible.
To quote the Good Book makes me liable.

We can elect a pregnant Senior Queen,
And the 'unwed daddy,' our Senior King.
It's 'inappropriate' to teach right from wrong.
We're taught that such 'judgments' do not belong.

We can get our condoms and birth controls,
Study witchcraft, vampires, and totem poles.
But the Ten Commandments are not allowed,
No word of God must reach this crowd.

It's scary here I must confess,
When chaos reigns the school's a mess.
So, Lord, this silent plea I make:
Should I be shot; My soul please take!
Amen

Contributed by Richard Sandford
10/09/2023

Lotsa Thoughts - Alphabetized

~ 33% say they won't have money to cover their holiday spending...Those people are called Congress.

~ A man's best friend is his dog. That's assuming you want a friend who messes on your carpet and drools on your newspaper.

~ A mother can touch a whole generation just by loving her own child well.

~ A physician once said: "The best medicine for humans is love." Someone asked, "What if it doesn't work?" He smiled and said: "Increase the dose."

~ A rumor without a leg to stand on will manage to get around some other way.

~ A veteran is someone who, at one point in their life, wrote a blank check made payable to The United States of America for an amount up to and including their life.

~ A word to the wise is unnecessary.

~ Advice is like castor oil - easy enough to give, but dreadfully uneasy to take.

~ All I want is a chance to prove that winning the lottery won't solve all my problems.

~ At what age do you go from being disrespectful to your elders, to being someone who thinks
"the young people today show no respect"?

~ Birthdays are good for you ... the more
you have the longer you live.

~ Did Adam and Eve ever have a date?
No, but they had an apple.

~ Do not believe in miracles...rely on them.

~ Dogs believe they are humans. Cats believe they are God.

~ Don't trust atoms...they make up everything.

~ Drive defensively. Buy a tank.

~ Farmer wisdom: Life is simpler when
you plow around the stumps.

~ Fish: an aquatic creature that grows rap-
idly between the time it spits a hook and the
time the angler describes it to his friends.

~ Football is not a contact sport; it is a collision sport. Dancing is a contact sport.

~ How come all the instruments seeking intelligent
life in the universe are pointed away from Earth?

~ I don't have gray hair. I have "wisdom highlights."

~ I don't need anger management. I need people to stop making me mad!

~ I don't trip over things, I do random gravity checks!

~ I have joined the Anti-Crastination
League. We are going Pro soon.

~ I misplaced my dictionary. Now I'm at a loss for words.

~ I tried to exercise, but I was allergic to it. My
skin flushed and my heart raced. I got sweaty
and short of breath. Very dangerous.

~ I want one of those jobs where people ask,
"Do you actually get paid to do this??"

~ I'd like to be the ideal mother, but I'm
too busy raising my kids.

~ I'm going to retire and live off of my savings.
Not sure what I'll do the second week.

~ I'm writing a book about reverse psychology. Don't buy it.

~ I've learned that even when I have
pains, I don't have to be one.

~ If evolution is true, why do moth-
ers still only have one pair of hands?

~ If someone says something unkind about me,
I must live so that no one will believe it.

~ If you aim at nothing, you'll hit it every time.

~ If you lined up all the cars in the world end to end,
someone would be stupid enough to try to pass
them, five or six at a time, on a hill, in the fog.

~ If you think nothing is impossible, try slamming a revolving door.

~ It's hard to gain a toehold if you're acting like a heel.

~ Last year I joined a support group for procrastinators. We haven't met yet.

~ Let God be God. He will be anyway.

~ Life isn't about how fast you run, or how high you climb; it's about how well you bounce.

~ Lord grant me the strength to accept the things I cannot change, the courage to change the things I can and the friends to post my bail when I finally snap.

~ Many folks who brag about being "young at heart" are quite older in other places.

~ Maybe there would be fewer collisions if the manufacturers give their car models less aggressive names, such as Kitten, Bunny Rabbit, and Feather Duster.

~ My people skills are just fine. It's my tolerance to idiots that needs work.

~ Never be ashamed to admit you are in the wrong - it's just another way to say you are wiser today than yesterday.

~ No one will ever win the battle of the sexes. There's too much fraternizing with the enemy.

~ Of course I talk to myself, sometimes I need expert advice.

~ Old age is coming at a really bad time!

~ On your birthday, send a thank you card to your mom.

~ Politicians should wear uniforms like NASCAR
drivers so we could identify their sponsors.

~ Progress always involves risks. You can't steal second base and keep your foot on first.

~ Q: What's green, fuzzy, and if it fell out of a
tree it would kill you? A: A pool table.

~ *Quando Omni Flunkus Moritai* (When
all else fails, play dead)

~ Read something no one else is reading, think something no
one else is thinking, and do something no one else is doing.

~ Stay away from negative people. They
have a problem for every solution.

~ Sure, you can't take it with you -- but you can
stash it where no other jerk can find it.

~ The best thing to spend on your children is time.

~ The biggest lie I tell myself is "I don't need
to write that down, I'll remember it."

~ The biggest problem with the younger generation
these days is that I don't belong to it any more.

~ The great thing about living in a small town is that when
you don't know what you're doing, someone else does.

~ The kids text me "plz" which is shorter than please.
I text back "no" which is shorter than "yes."

~ The older we get, the fewer things seem
worth waiting in line for.

~ The shortest distance between two points
depends on how far apart they are.

~ The surest way to save face is to keep the lower part shut.

~ The things that come to those who wait will be
the things left by those who got there first.

~ THINK! It gives you something to do
while the computer is down.

~ Travel is very educational. I can now say
"Kaopectate" in seven different languages.

~ Two antennae met on a roof, fell in love and got
married. Their wedding ceremony wasn't fancy.
The reception, however, was excellent.

~ Warning: Dates on calendar are closer than they appear.

~ Wasting time is an important part of life.

~ We have 35 million laws to enforce the Ten Commandments.

~ We have enough youth. How about a fountain of SMART?

~ Wealthy people miss one of life's greatest thrills: Making the last car payment.

~ Well, this day was a total waste of make-up.

~ What hair color do they put on the driver's license of a bald man?

~ What if the Hokey-Pokey really IS what it's all about?

~ What would you rather have? No short-term
memory or . . . I forget the question.

~ When a DJ drives under an overpass, does his voice fade out?

~ When all else fails, read the instructions.

~ When at a loss for the right word to say, try silence.

~ When everything's coming your way,
you're in the wrong lane.

~ When I die, I want to go peacefully like my grandfather did-
-in his sleep. Not screaming like the passengers in his car.

~ When it rains, why don't sheep shrink?

~ When the going gets tough, everyone leaves.

~ Wherever I go, the world's worst drivers follow me there.

~ With some people you spend an evening. With others you invest it.

~ Wouldn't it be great if we could put ourselves in the dryer for ten minutes and come
out wrinkle-free and three sizes smaller?

~ You can tell a lot about a man by the way he han-
dles these three things: a rainy day, lost lug-
gage, and tangled Christmas tree lights.

~ You don't have an attitude problem. They
just have a perception problem.

~ You haven't had enough coffee until you can
thread a sewing machine while it's running.

Contributed by Judy Flahiff
10-03-2023

Make the Chili!

A good friend of mine unexpectedly lost his wife.

A couple months later we were golfing together, chatting about nothing. He asked what my dinner plans were, and I told him that wifey wanted my homemade chili and cornbread, but I didn't feel like stopping at the store.

We golfed a few more minutes when he quietly said, "Make the chili."

It took me a few minutes to realize we were no longer talking about dinner. It was about going out of your way to do something for someone you love because at any moment, they could unexpectedly be taken from you.

So today I'm sharing with you that wisdom handed to me by my dear friend. I've thought of it many times since that day…

The next time someone you love wants you to go for a walk or watch a football game or play a board game or just put your phone down and give them your undivided attention, just do it. "Make the chili!"

Contributed by Marshall Nestor
4/27/2024

Odds & Ends

(Not checked for veracity)

<u>Why do men's clothes have buttons on the right while women's clothes have buttons on the left?</u>

Because:
When buttons were invented, they were very expensive and worn primarily by the rich. Since most people are right-handed, it is easier to push buttons on the right through holes on the left. Because wealthy women were dressed by maids, dressmakers put the buttons on the maid's right! And that's where women's buttons have remained since.

>———<<< ● >>>———<

<u>Why do ships and aircraft use 'mayday' as their call for help?</u>

Because:
This comes from the French word m'aidez -meaning 'help me' -- and is pronounced, approximately, 'mayday.'

>———<<< ● >>>———<

<u>Why are zero scores in tennis called 'love'?</u>

Because:
In France, where tennis became popular, the round zero on the scoreboard looked like an egg and was called 'l'oeuf,' which is French for 'the egg.' When tennis was introduced in the US, Americans (mis)pronounced it 'love.'

Why do X's at the end of a letter signify kisses?

Because:
In the Middle Ages, when many people were unable to read or write, documents were often signed using an X. Kissing the X represented an oath to fulfill obligations specified in the document. The X and the kiss eventually became synonymous.

Why is shifting responsibility to someone else called 'passing the buck'?

Because:
In card games, it was once customary to pass an item, called a buck, from player to player to indicate whose turn it was to deal. If a player did not wish to assume the responsibility of dealing, he would 'pass the buck' to the next player.

Why do people clink their glasses before drinking a toast?

Because:
It used to be common for someone to try to kill an enemy by offering him a poisoned drink. To prove to a guest that a drink was safe, it became customary for a guest to pour a small amount of his drink into the glass of the host. Both men would drink it simultaneously. When a guest trusted his host, he would only touch or clink the host's glass with his own.

<u>Why are people in the public eye said to be 'in the limelight'?</u>

Because:
Invented in 1825, limelight was used in lighthouses and theaters by burning a cylinder of lime which produced a brilliant light. In the theatre, a performer 'in the limelight' was the center of attention.

>———‹‹‹ ● ›››———‹

<u>Why is someone who is feeling great 'on cloud nine'?</u>

Because:
Types of clouds are numbered according to the altitudes they attain, with nine being the highest cloud. If someone is said to be on cloud nine, that person is floating well above worldly cares.

>———‹‹‹ ● ›››———‹

<u>Why in golf, where did the term 'Caddie' come from?</u>

Because:
When Mary Queen of Scots went to France as a young girl, Louis, King of France, learned that she loved the Scots game 'golf.' He had the first course outside of Scotland built for her enjoyment. To make sure she was properly chaperoned (and guarded) while she played, Louis hired cadets from a military school to accompany her. Mary liked this a lot and when returned to Scotland (not a very good idea in the long run), she took the practice with her.

In French, the word cadet is pronounced 'ca-day' and the Scots changed it into 'caddie.'

>———‹‹‹ ● ›››———‹

<u>Why are many coin collection jar banks shaped like pigs?</u>

Because:
Long ago, dishes and cookware in Europe were made of a dense orange clay called 'pygg'. When people saved coins in jars made of this clay, the jars became known as 'pygg banks.' When an English potter misunderstood the word, he made a container that resembled a pig. And it caught on.

W.G. Williams
March 26, 2013

Our Founders' Discussions Over the Separation of Church and State

"If I could conceive that the general government might ever be so administered as to render the liberty of conscience insecure, I beg you will be persuaded, that no one would be more zealous than myself to establish effectual barriers against the horrors of spiritual tyranny, and every species of religious persecution."
- George Washington, letter to the United Baptist Chamber of Virginia (1789)

"Question with boldness even the existence of a God; because, if there be one, he must more approve of the homage of reason, then that of blindfolded fear."
- Thomas Jefferson, letter to Peter Carr (1787)

"In regard to religion, mutual toleration in the different professions thereof is what all good and candid minds in all ages have ever practiced, and both by precept and example inculcated on mankind."
- Samuel Adams, *The Rights of the Colonists* (1771)

"Persecution is not an original feature in any religion; but it is always the strongly marked feature of all religions established by law. Take away the law-establishment, and every religion re-assumes its original benignity."
- Thomas Paine, *The Rights of Man* (1791)

"Congress has no power to make any religious establishments."
- Roger Sherman, Congress (1789)

"The way to see by faith is to shut the eye of reason."
- Benjamin Franklin, *Poor Richard's Almanack* (1758)

"I contemplate with sovereign reverence that act of the whole American people build a wall of separation between Church & State."
- Thomas Jefferson, letter to the Danbury Baptists (1802)

"To argue with a man who has renounced the use of reason is like administering medicine to the dead."
- Thomas Paine, *The American Crisis No. V* (1776)

"Our civil rights have no dependence on our religious opinions, any more than our opinions in physics or geometry."
- Thomas Jefferson, *A Bill for Establishing Religious Freedom* (1779)

"Christian establishments tend to great ignorance and corruption, all of which facilitate the execution of mischievous projects."
- James Madison, letter to William Bradford, Jr. (1774)

"There is nothing which can better deserve our patronage than the promotion of science and literature. Knowledge is in every country the surest basis of public happiness."
- George Washington, address to Congress (1790)

"During almost fifteen centuries has the legal establishment of Christianity been on trial. What has been its fruits? More or less, in all places, pride and indolence in the clergy; ignorance and servility in the laity; in both, superstition, *bigotry and persecution."*
- *James Madison, General Assembly of the Commonwealth of Virginia (1785)*

W.G. Williams
6/8/2023

Out of Gas

Returning after traveling a great distance by car to get medical supplies for their small clinic, two nuns ran out of gas quite literally, "in the middle of nowhere." They knew the area well; no gas for miles in either direction. Not wanting to leave the supplies and not wanting to be separated, they began to pray.

Just then a gas tanker stopped, and the driver asked, "Sisters, what is wrong?"

They explained their gas gauge was faulty and they had run out of gas.

He replied that his tanker was empty and he was on his way to load fuel for one of his routes. But on inspection he found he had a little in one of his lines; however, he had no bucket to catch the remaining tidbit of fuel.

"Bed pans," replied one sister. "We have bed pans!"

With that, they got out the bed pans and gratefully caught all of the last little bit of gas in the tanker.

Then the driver said, "Sisters, I'm short on time and I must go!"

The sisters thanked him and poured the gas into the car. As they were pouring in the last little bit, a highway patrolman pulled up got out of the patrol car and stared in disbelief.

"Sisters, I've no idea what you've done, but I sure admire your faith!"

Contributed by Tom Benner
2/20/2009

Owls Get High with A Little Help from Their Friends

Contributed by Burt Kempner
1/24/2019

Perks of Being a Senior Citizen

1.
Kidnappers are not very interested in you.

2.
In a hostage situation, you are likely to be released first.

3.
No one expects you to run -- anywhere.

4.
People call at 9 PM (or 9 AM) and ask, "Did I wake you?"

5.
People no longer view you as a hypochondriac.

6.
There is nothing left to learn the hard way.

7.
Things you buy now won't wear out.

8.
You can eat supper at 4 PM.

9.
You can't live without your glasses.

10.
You get into heated arguments about pension plans.

11.
You no longer think of speed limits as a challenge.

12.
You quit trying to hold your stomach in no
matter who walks into the room.

13.
You sing along with elevator music.

14.
Your eyes won't get much worse.

15.
Your investment in health insurance is finally beginning to pay off.

16.
Your joints are more accurate meteorologists
than the national weather service.

17.
Your secrets are safe with your friends because
they can't remember them either.

18.
Your supply of brain cells is finally down to a manageable size.

19.
You can't remember who sent you this list.

And you notice these are all in bigger print for your convenience.

Forward this to everyone you can remember right now!

AND THE MOST IMPORTANT THING:

Never, NEVER, NEVER, under any circumstances, take
a sleeping pill, and a laxative on the same night!

Contributed by Tim Butler
4/10/2024

Picturesque Ohio...

Dear Diary: Aug. 12 –
Moved into our new home in Ohio. It is so beautiful here. The hills and river valleys are so picturesque. I have a beautiful old oak tree in my front yard. Can hardly wait to see the change in the seasons. This is truly God's Country.

Dear Diary: Oct. 14 –
Ohio is such a gorgeous place to live, one of the real special places on Earth. The leaves are turning a multitude of different colors. I love all of the shades of reds, oranges and yellows, they are so bright. I want to walk through all of the beautiful hills and spot some white tail deer. They are so graceful; certainly, they must be the most peaceful creatures on Earth. This must be paradise.

Dear Diary: Nov. 11 –
Deer season opens this week. I can't imagine why anyone would want to shoot these elegant animals. They are the very symbol of peace and tranquility here in Ohio. I hope it snows soon. I love it here!

Dear Diary: Dec. 2 –
It snowed last night. I woke to the usual wonderful sight: everything covered in a beautiful blanket of white. The oak tree is magnificent. It looks like a postcard. We went out and swept the snow from the steps and driveway. The air is so crisp, clean and refreshing. We had a snowball fight. I won, and the snowplow came down the street. He must have gotten too close to the driveway because we had to go out and shovel the end of the driveway again. What a beautiful place. Nature in harmony…I love it here!

Dear Diary: Dec. 12 –
More snow last night. I love it! The plow did his cute little trick again. What a rascal. A winter wonderland. I love it here!

Dear Diary: Dec. 19 –
More snow - couldn't get out of the driveway to get to work in time. I'm exhausted from all of the shoveling. And that snowplow!

Dear Diary: Dec. 21 –
More of that white shit coming down. I've got blisters on my hands and a kink in my back. I think that the snowplow driver waits around the corner until I'm done shoveling the driveway. Asshole.

Dear Diary: Dec. 25 –
White Christmas? More freakin' snow. If I ever get my hands on the guy who drives that snowplow, I swear I'll castrate him. And why don't they use more salt on these roads to melt this crap??

Dear Diary: Dec. 28 –
It hasn't stopped snowing since Christmas. I have been inside since then, except of course when that SOB "Snowplow Harry" comes by. Can't go anywhere, cars are buried up to the windows. Weatherman says to expect another 10 inches. Do you have any idea how many shovelsful 10 inches is??

Dear Diary: Jan. 1 –
Happy New Year? The way it's coming down, it won't melt until the 4th of July! The snowplow got stuck down the road and the shithead actually had the balls to come and ask to borrow a shovel! I told him I'd broken six already this season.

Dear Diary: Jan. 4 –
Finally got out of the house. We went to the store to get some food and a damn deer ran out in front of my car and I hit the SOB. It did $3,000 in damage to the car. Those beasts ought to be killed. The hunters should have a longer season if you ask me.

Dear Diary: Jan. 27 –
Warmed up a little and rained today. The rain turned the snow into ice and the weight of it broke the main limb of the oak tree in the front yard and it went through the roof. I should have cut that old piece of shit into fireplace wood when I had the chance.

Dear Diary: May 23 –
Took my car to the local garage. Would you believe the whole underside of the car is rusted away from all of that damn salt they dump on the road? Car looks like a bashed up, heap of rusted cow shit.

Dear Diary: June 10 –
Sold the car, the house, and moved to Florida. I can't imagine why anyone in their freakin' mind would ever want to live in the God forsaken State of Ohio!

Contributed by Barbara Stretavski
2/2/2009

Pray For Leroy...

The preacher said, *"Anyone who wants to be prayed over, please come forward to the front by the altar."*

With that, Leroy got in line, and when it was his turn, the Preacher asked, *"Leroy, what do you want me to pray about for you?"*

Leroy replied, *"Preacher, I need you to pray for help with my hearing."*

The preacher put one finger of one hand in Leroy's ear, placed his other hand on top of his head, and then prayed and prayed and prayed. He prayed a "blue streak" for him and the whole congregation joined in with great enthusiasm.

After a few minutes, the preacher removed his hands, stood back and asked, *"Leroy, how is your hearing now?"*

Leroy answered, *"I don't know. It ain't 'til next week."*

Contributed by E.W. Hallford
3/9/2011

Puns for Educated Minds...

1. The roundest knight at King Arthur's round table was Sir Cumference. He acquired his size from too much pi.

2. I thought I saw an eye doctor on an Alaskan island, but it turned out to be an optical Aleutian.

3. She was only a whiskey maker, but he loved her still.

4. A rubber band pistol was confiscated from algebra class because it was a weapon of math disruption.

5. The butcher backed into the meat grinder and got a little behind in his work.

6. No matter how much you push the envelope, it'll still be stationery.

7. A dog gave birth to puppies near the road and was cited for littering.

8. A grenade thrown into a kitchen in France would result in Linoleum Blownapart.

9. Two silkworms had a race. They ended up in a tie.

10. Time flies like an arrow. Fruit flies like a banana.

11. A hole has been found in the nudist camp wall. The police are looking into it.

12. Atheism is a non-prophet organization.

13. Two hats were hanging on a hat rack in the hallway. One hat said to the other, "You stay here; I'll go on a head."

14. I wondered why the baseball kept getting bigger. Then it hit me.

15. A sign on the lawn at a drug rehab center said: "Keep off the Grass."

16. A small boy swallowed some coins and was taken to a hospital. When His grandmother telephoned to ask how he was, a nurse said, "No change yet."

17. A chicken crossing the road is poultry in motion.

18. The short fortune-teller who escaped from prison was a small medium at large.

19. The soldier who survived mustard gas and pepper spray is now a seasoned veteran.

20. A backward poet writes inverse.

21. In democracy it's your vote that counts. In feudalism it's your count that votes.

22. When cannibals ate a missionary, they got a taste of religion.

Contributed by Ron Gargasz
5/12/2009

Quotes From British Military Annual Staff Appraisals

1. His men would follow him anywhere - but only out of curiosity.

2. I would not breed from this Officer.

3. This man is depriving a village somewhere of its idiot.

4. This Officer can be likened to a small puppy - he runs around excitedly, leaving little messes for other people to clean up.

5. This Officer is really not so much of a has-been … more of a definitely won't-be.

6. When she opens her mouth, it seems only to change whichever foot was previously in there.

7. Couldn't organize 50% leave in a 2-man submarine.

8. He has carried out each and every one of his duties to his entire satisfaction.

9. He would be out of his depth in a car park puddle.

10. Technically sound but socially impossible.

11. The occasional flashes of adequacy are marred by an attitude of apathy and indifference.

12. When he joined my ship this Officer was something of a granny; since then, he has aged considerably.

13. This Medical Officer has used my ship to carry his genitals from port to port, and my officers to carry him from bar to bar.

14. This Officer reminds me very much of a gyroscope, always spinning around at a frantic pace but not really going anywhere.

15. Since my last report he has reached rock bottom and has started to dig.

16. She sets low personal standards and then consistently fails to achieve them.

17. He has the wisdom of youth and the energy of old age.

18. This Officer should go far and the sooner he starts, the better.

19. In my opinion this pilot should not be authorized to fly below 250 feet.

20. The only ship I would recommend for this man is citizenship.

21. Couldn't organize a woodpecker's picnic in Sherwood Forest.

22. Works well when under constant supervision and when cornered like a rat in a trap.

23. Not the sharpest knife in the drawer.

24. Gates are down, the lights are flashing but the train isn't coming.

25. Has two brains; one is lost and the other is out looking for it.

26. If he were any more stupid, he'd have to be watered twice a week.

27. Got into the gene pool while the lifeguard wasn't watching.

28. If you stand close enough to him, you can hear the ocean.

29. It's hard to believe that he beat 1,000,000 other sperm.

30. A room temperature IQ.

31. Got a full 6-pack but lacks the plastic thingy to hold it all together.

32. A gross ignoramus … 144 times worse than an ordinary ignoramus.

33. He has a photographic memory but has the lens cover glued on.

34. He has been working with glue too long.

35. When his IQ reaches 50, he should sell.

36. This man hasn't got enough grey matter to sole the flip-flop of a one-legged budgie.

37. If two people are talking and one looks bored, he's the other one.

38. One-celled organisms would out score him in an IQ test.

39. He donated his body to science before he was done using it.

40. Fell out of the stupid tree and hit every branch on the way down.

41. He's so dense light bends around him.

42. If brains were taxed, he'd get a rebate.

43. Some drink from the fountain of knowledge; he only gargled.

44. Takes him 1½ hours to watch 60 minutes.

45. Wheel is turning but the hamster is long dead

Contributed by Julius Graw
10-10-2023

Ronald Reagan's Sayings

"Here's my strategy on the Cold War: We win, they lose."
"There are no constraints on the human mind, no walls around the human spirit, no barriers to our progress except those we ourselves erect."

"Some people wonder all their lives if they've made a difference. The Marines don't have that problem."

"There are no such things as limits to growth, because there are no limits to the human capacity for intelligence, imagination, and wonder."

"The most terrifying words in the English language are, I'm from the government and I'm here to help."

"Of the four wars in my lifetime, none came about because the U.S. was too strong."

"I have wondered at times about what the Ten Commandments would have looked like if Moses had run them through the U.S. Congress."

"The taxpayer: That's someone who works for the federal government but doesn't have to take the civil service examination."

"Government is like a baby: An alimentary canal with a big appetite at one end and no sense of responsibility at the other."

"The nearest thing to eternal life we will ever see on this earth is a government program."

"It has been said that politics is the second oldest profession. I have learned that it bears a striking resemblance to the first."

"Government's view of the economy could be summed up in a few short phrases: If it moves, tax it. If it keeps moving, regulate it. And if it stops moving, subsidize it."

"Politics is not a bad profession. If you succeed, there are many rewards; if you disgrace yourself, you can always write a book."

"No arsenal, or no weapon in the arsenals of the world, is as formidable as the will and moral courage of free men and women."

"If we ever forget that we're one nation under God, then we will be a nation gone under."

Contributed by Renee Bernstein
10/20/2023

A REALLY Bad Day...

A guy was sitting at the bar just staring at his drink for half an hour when a big, trouble-making biker stepped next to him, grabbed his drink, gulped it down in one swig and then turned to the guy with a menacing stare as if to say, "What'cha gonna do about it?"

The poor guy started crying.

"Come on man, I was just giving you a hard time," the biker said. "I didn't think you'd CRY. I can't stand to see a man crying."

"This is the worst day of my life," he said between sobs. "I can't do anything right. I overslept and was late to an important meeting, so my boss fired me. When I went to the parking lot, I found my car was stolen and I don't have any insurance. I left my wallet in the cab I took home. I found my wife in bed with the gardener and then my dog bit me.

So, I came to this bar trying to work up the courage to put an end to my life, and then you showed up and drank the damn poison..."

Contributed by Bubba & Bonnie Mehling
3/10/2009

Redneck Valentine

Collards is green,
My dog's name is Blue
And I'm so lucky to have
A sweet thang like you.
Yore hair is like corn silk
A-flapping in the breeze.
Softer than Blue's
And without all them fleas.

You move like the bass,
Which excite me in May.
You ain't got no scales
But I luv you anyway.
Yo're as satisfy'n as okry
A-fry'n in the pan.
Yo're as fragrant as "snuff"
Right out of the can.

You have some'a yore teeth,
For which I am proud;
I hold my head high
When we're in a crowd.
On special occasions,
When you shave under yore arms,
Well, I'm in hawg heaven,
And awed by yore charms.

W.G. Williams

Still them fellers at work,
They all want to know,
What I did to deserve
Such a purdy, young doe.
Like a good roll of duct tape,
Yo're there fer yore man,
To patch up life's troubles
And fix what you can.

Yo're as cute as a junebug
A-buzzin' overhead.
You ain't mean like those far ants
I found in my bed.
Cut from the best cloth
Like a plaid flannel shirt,
You spark up my life
More than a fresh load of dirt.

When you hold me real tight
Like a padded gunrack,
My life is complete;
Ain't nuttin' I lack.
Yore complexion, it's perfection,
Like the best vinyl sidin'.
Despite all the years,
Yore age, it keeps hidin'.

Me 'n' you's like a Moon Pie
With a RC cold drank,
We go together
Like a skunk goes with stank.
Some men,
They buy chocolate for Valentine's Day;
They git it at Wal-Mart,
It's romantic that way.

Some men git roses
On that special day
From the cooler at Kroger.
That's impressive," I say.
Some men buy fine diamonds
From a flea market booth.
"Diamonds are forever,"
They explain, suave and couth.

But for this man, honey,
These won't do.
Cause you're too special,
You sweet thang you.
I got you a gift,
Without taste nor odor,
More useful than diamonds......
IT'S A NEW TROLL'N MOTOR!!

Contributed by Jamie Gillett
1/14/2006

Retarded Grandparents

After Christmas, a teacher asked her young pupils how they spent their holiday away from school. One child wrote the following:

We always used to spend the holidays with Grandma and Grandpa. They used to live in a big brick house, but Grandpa got retarded and they moved to Arizona. Now they live in a tin box and have rocks painted green to look like grass.

They ride around on their bicycles and wear name tags because they don't know who they are anymore. They go to a building called a wrecked center, but they must have got it fixed because it is okay now, and do exercises there, but they don't do them very well. There is a swimming pool too, but in it, they all jump up and down with hats on.

At their gate, there is a doll house with a little old man sitting in it. He watches all day so nobody can escape. Sometimes they sneak out. They go cruising in their golf carts. Nobody there cooks, they just eat out. And they eat the same thing every night: Early Birds.

Some of the people can't get out past the man in the doll house. The ones who do get out, bring food back to the wrecked center and call it potluck.

My Grandma says that Grandpa worked all his life to earn his retardment and says I should work hard so I can be retarded someday too. When I earn early retardment, I want to be the man in the doll house. Then I'll let people out so they can visit their grandchildren.

Contributed by Ron Gargasz
3/23/2006

Rules for Eating at Christmas...

1. Avoid carrot sticks. Anyone who puts carrots on a holiday buffet table knows nothing of the Christmas spirit. In fact, if you see carrots, leave immediately. Go next door, where they're serving rum balls.

2. Drink as much eggnog as you can. And quickly. Like fine single-malt scotch, it's rare. In fact, it's even rarer than single-malt scotch. You can't find it any other time of year but now. So drink up! Who cares that it has 10,000 calories in every sip? It's not as if you're going to turn into an eggnog-aholic or something. It's a treat. Enjoy it. Have one for me. Have two. It's later than you think. It's Christmas!

3. If something comes with gravy, use it. That's the whole point of gravy. Gravy does not stand alone. Pour it on. Make a volcano out of your mashed potatoes. Fill it with gravy. Eat the volcano. Repeat.

4. As for mashed potatoes, always ask if they're made with skim milk or whole milk. If it's skim, pass. Why bother? It's like buying a sports car with an automatic transmission.

5. Do not have a snack before going to a party in an effort to control your eating. The whole point of going to a Christmas party is to eat other people's food for free. Lots of it. Hello?

6. Under no circumstances should you exercise between now and New Year's. You can do that in January when you have nothing else to do. This is the time for long naps, which you'll need after circling the buffet table while carrying a 10-pound plate of food and that vat of eggnog.

7. If you come across something really good at a buffet table, like frosted Christmas cookies in the shape and size of Santa, position yourself near them and don't budge. Have as many as you can before becoming the center of attention. They're like a beautiful pair of shoes. If you leave them behind, you're never going to see them again.

8. Same for pies. Apple. Pumpkin. Mincemeat. Have a slice of each. Or, if you don't like mincemeat, have two apples and one pumpkin. Always have three. When else do you get to have more than one dessert? Labor Day?

9. Did someone mention fruitcake? Granted, it's loaded with the mandatory celebratory calories, but avoid it at all cost. I mean, have some standards.

10. One final tip: If you don't feel terrible when you leave the party or get up from the table, you haven't been paying attention.

Reread tips; start over, but hurry, January is just around the corner.

Remember this motto to live by:

"Life should NOT be a journey to the grave with the intention of arriving safely in an attractive and well-preserved body, but rather to skid in sideways, chocolate in one hand, body thoroughly used up and totally worn out, and screaming, "WOO HOO what a ride!"
Merry Christmas everyone!

Contributed by Ron Heisler
12/17/2007

Sarah and Santa

A few years ago, a little boy and his grandmother came to see Santa at the McAllister Mall in Saint John. The child climbed up on his lap, holding a picture of a little girl.

"Who is this?" asked Santa, smiling. "Your friend?"

"Yes, Santa," he replied. "My sister, Sarah, is very sick," he said sadly.

Santa glanced over at the grandmother who was waiting nearby and saw her dabbing her eyes with a tissue. "She wanted to come with me to see you, oh, so very much, Santa!" the child exclaimed. "She misses you," he added softly.

Santa tried to be cheerful and to encourage a smile on the boy's face by asking him what he wanted Santa to bring him for Christmas.

When they finished their visit, the grandmother came over to help the child off his lap, and started to say something to Santa, but halted.

"What is it?" Santa asked warmly.

"Well, I know it's really too much to ask, Santa, but…" the old woman began, shooing her grandson over to one of Santa's elves to collect the little gift which Santa gave all his young visitors.

"The girl in the photograph… my granddaughter well, you see … she has leukemia and isn't expected to make it even through the holidays," she said through tear-filled eyes. "Is there any way, Santa, any possible way that you could come see Sarah? That's all she's asked for is to see Santa."

Santa blinked and swallowed hard and told the woman to leave information with his elves as to where Sarah was, and he would see what he could do.

Santa thought of little else the rest of that afternoon. He knew what he had to do. "What if it were MY child lying in that hospital bed, dying," he thought with a sinking heart, "This is the least I can do."

When Santa finished visiting with all the boys and girls that evening, he retrieved from his helper the name of the hospital where Sarah was staying. He asked Rick, the assistant location manager, how to get to the Hospital.

"Why?" Rick asked, with a puzzled look on his face.

Santa relayed to him the conversation with Sarah's grandmother earlier that day.

"C'mon...I'll take you there." Rick said softly. Rick drove them to the hospital and came inside with Santa. They found out which room Sarah was in. A pale Rick said he would wait out in the hall.

Santa quietly peeked into the room through the half-closed door and saw little Sarah in bed.

The room was full of what appeared to be her family; there was the grandmother and the girl's brother he had met earlier that day. A woman whom he guessed was Sarah's mother stood by the bed, gently pushing Sarah's thin hair off her forehead. And another woman who he discovered later was Sarah's aunt, sat in a chair near the bed with a weary sad look on her face. They were talking quietly, and Santa could sense the warmth and closeness of the family, and their love and concern for Sarah.

Taking a deep breath, and forcing a smile on his face, Santa entered the room, bellowing a hearty, "Ho, Ho, Ho!"

"Santa!" shrieked little Sarah, weakly as she tried to escape her bed and IV tubes to run to him.

Santa rushed to her side and gave her a warm hug.

A child was the tender age of his own son, and she gazed up at him with wonder and excitement. Her skin was pale, and her short tresses bore telltale bald patches from the effects of chemotherapy. But all he saw when he looked at her was a pair of huge blue eyes. His heart melted, and he had to force himself to choke back tears.

Though his eyes were riveted upon Sarah's face, he could hear the gasps and quiet sobbing of the women in the room.

As he and Sarah began talking, the family crept quietly to the bedside one by one, squeezing Santa's shoulder or his hand gratefully, whispering "Thank you" as they gazed sincerely at him with shining eyes.

Santa and Sarah talked and talked, and she told him excitedly all the toys she wanted for Christmas, assuring him she'd been a very good girl that year.

As their time together dwindled, Santa felt led in his spirit to pray for Sarah and asked for permission from the girl's mother. She nodded in agreement and the entire family circled around Sarah's bed, holding hands. Santa looked intensely at Sarah and asked her if she believed in angels.

"Oh, yes, Santa... I do!" she exclaimed.

"Well, I'm going to ask angels watch over you." he said. Laying one hand on the child's head, Santa closed his eyes and prayed. He asked that, God touch Sarah and heal her body from this disease. He asked that angels minister to her, watch and keep her. And when he finished praying, still with eyes closed, he started singing, softly, "Silent Night, Holy Night....all is calm, all is bright."

The family joined in, still holding hands, smiling at Sarah, and crying tears of hope, tears of joy for this moment, as Sarah beamed at them all.

When the song ended, Santa sat on the side of the bed again and held Sarah's frail, small hands in his own. "Now, Sarah," he said authoritatively, "you have a job to do, and that is to concentrate on getting well. I want you to have fun playing with your friends this summer, and I expect to see you at my house at McAllister Mall this time next year!"

He knew it was risky proclaiming that to this little girl who had terminal cancer, but he "had" too. He had to give her the greatest gift he could -- not dolls or games or toys -- but the gift of HOPE.

"Yes, Santa!" Sarah exclaimed, her eyes bright.

He leaned down and kissed her on the forehead and left the room. Out in the hall, the minute Santa's eyes met Rick's, a look passed between them, and they wept unashamedly.

Sarah's mother and grandmother slipped out of the room quickly and rushed to Santa's side to thank him.

"My only child is the same age as Sarah," he explained quietly. "This is the least I could do." They nodded with understanding and hugged him.

One year later, Santa was again back on the set in Saint John for his six-week, seasonal job which he really loves to do. Several weeks went by and then one day a child came up to sit on his lap.

"Hi, Santa! Remember me?"

"Of course, I do," Santa proclaimed (as he always does), smiling down at her. After all, the secret to being a "good" Santa is to always make each child feel as if they are the "only" child in the world at that moment.

"You came to see me in the hospital last year!"

Santa's jaw dropped. Tears immediately sprang in his eyes, and he grabbed this little miracle and held her to his chest. "Sarah!" he exclaimed.

He scarcely recognized her, for her hair was long and silky and her cheeks were rosy -- much different from the little girl he had visited just a year before. He looked over and saw Sarah's mother and grandmother on the sidelines smiling and waving and wiping their eyes.

That was the best Christmas ever for Santa Claus. He had witnessed --and been blessed to be instrumental in bringing about -- this miracle of hope. This precious little child was healed. Cancer-free. Alive and well.

He silently looked up to Heaven and humbly whispered, "Thank you, Father. 'Tis a very, Merry Christmas!"

Contributed by Fred Schroeder
12/29/2022

A Scam at Home Depot...

A 'heads up' for those men who may be regular Home Depot customers. This one caught me by surprise.

Over the last month I became a victim of a clever scam while out shopping. Simply going out to get supplies has turned out to be quite traumatic. Don't be naive enough to think it couldn't happen to you or your friends.

Here's how the scam works:

Two seriously good-looking 20-21 year-old girls come over to your car as you're packing your shopping into the trunk. They both start wiping your windshield with a rag and Windex with their breasts almost falling out of their skimpy T-shirts. It's impossible not to look

When you thank them and offer them a tip, they say "No" and instead ask you for a ride to McDonalds.

You agree and they get into the back seat. On the way, they start undressing. Then one of them climbs over into the front seat and starts crawling all over you while the other one steals your wallet.

I had my wallet stolen November 4th, 9th, 10th, twice on the 15th, 17th, 20th, 24th & 29th. Also, December 1st & 4th, twice on the 8th, 16th, 23rd, 26th & 30th, three times last Monday and very likely again this upcoming weekend.

So tell your friends to be careful.

P.S. Walmart has wallets on sale for 2.99 each.

Contributed by Bubba & Bonnie Mehling
1/29/2009

Selling a Clunker...

Judi tried to sell her old car. She was having a lot of problems selling it because the car had 250,000 miles on it. One day, she told her problem to a friend she worked with at a salon. Her friend told her, "There is a possibility to make the car easier to sell, but it's not legal."

"That doesn't matter," replied Judi, "if only I can sell the car."

"Okay," said Judi's friend. "Here is the address of a friend of mine. He owns a car repair shop. Tell him I sent you and he will turn the counter in your car back to 50,000 miles. Then it shouldn't be a problem selling your car."

The following weekend, Judi made the trip to the mechanic. Two weeks later the friend asked Judi, "Did you sell your car?"

"No," replied Judi, "why should I? It only has 50,000 miles on it!"

Contributed by Tom Benner
8/20/2010

Short Takes on Ageing...

--- Reporters interviewing a 104-year-old woman: "And what do you think is the best thing about being 104?" the reporter asked.

She simply replied, "No peer pressure."

+ + + + + + +

--- The nice thing about being senile is you can hide your own Easter eggs.

+ + + + + + +

--- Just before the funeral services, the undertaker came up to the very elderly widow and asked, "How old was your husband?"

"98," she replied. "Two years older than me."

"So you're 96," the undertaker commented.

She responded, "Hardly worth going home, isn't it?

+ + + + + + +

--- I've sure gotten old.! I've had two bypass surgeries, a hip replacement, new knees. Fought prostate cancer and diabetes. I'm half blind, can't hear anything quieter than a jet engine, take 40 different medications that make me dizzy, winded, and subject to blackouts. Have bouts with dementia. Have poor circulation; hardly feel my hands and feet anymore. Can't remember if I'm 85 or 92. Have lost all my friends. But thank God, I still have my driver's license.

+ + + + + + +

--- A 97-year-old man goes into his doctor's office and says, "Doc, I want my sex drive lowered."

"Sir," replied the doctor, "you're 97 Don't you think your sex drive is all in your head?"

"You're damned right it is!" replied the old man. "That's why I want it lowered!"

+ + + + + + +

--- An elderly woman decided to prepare her will and told her preacher she had two final requests. First, she wanted to be cremated, and second, she wanted her ashes scattered over Wal-Mart.

"Wal-Mart?" the preacher exclaimed. "Why Wal-Mart?"

"Then I'll be sure my daughters visit me twice a week."

+ + + + + + +

---My memory's not as sharp as it used to be. Also, my memory's not as sharp as it used to be.

+ + + + + + +

--- Know how to prevent sagging? Just eat till the wrinkles fill out.

+ + + + + + +

---I've still got it, but nobody wants to see it.

+ + + + + + +

---I'm getting into swing dancing. Not on purpose. Some parts of my body are just prone to swinging.

+ + + + + + +

---It's scary when you start making the same noises as your coffeemaker.

+ + + + + + + +

---The good news is that even as we get older, guys still look at our boobs. The bad news is they have to squat down first.

+ + + + + + + +

---These days about half the stuff in my shopping cart says, "For fast relief."

+ + + + + + + +

---I've tried to find a suitable exercise video for women my age, but they haven't made one called "Buns of Putty."

+ + + + + + + +

---Don't think of it as getting hot flashes. Think of it as your inner child playing with matches.

+ + + + + + + +

---Don't let aging get you down. It's too hard to get back up!

+ + + + + + + +

--- Remember: You don't stop laughing because you grow old; you grow old because you stop laughing.

+ + + + + + + +

- --THE SENILITY PRAYER: Grant me the senility to forget the people I never liked anyway, the good fortune to run into the ones I do, and the eyesight to tell the difference.

Contributed by Gary Thornton
10/24/2005

Smiles for the Weekend

Every time a bird craps on my car, I eat a plate of wings on the front porch to show them what I'm capable of.

Decided to go for a walk on the beach and got freaked out when I thought I ran into a KKK meeting...turns out they're just closed beach umbrellas

ME: ALEXA, REMIND ME TO GO TO THE GYM.
ALEXA: I HAVE ADDED GIN TO YOUR SHOPPING LIST.
ME: CLOSE ENOUGH.

Things I'd rather do than watch The Grammys

NO TRESPASSING
WE'RE TIRED OF HIDING THE BODIES

IF YOU'RE BUYING A WATCH FROM AMAZON, BE WARNED. I LEARNED THE HARD WAY THAT IF IT SAYS YOU CAN SWIM WITH IT, THIS ONLY APPLIES IF YOU CAN ALREADY SWIM WITHOUT IT.

In case you didn't notice, I'm wearing the same dress!..

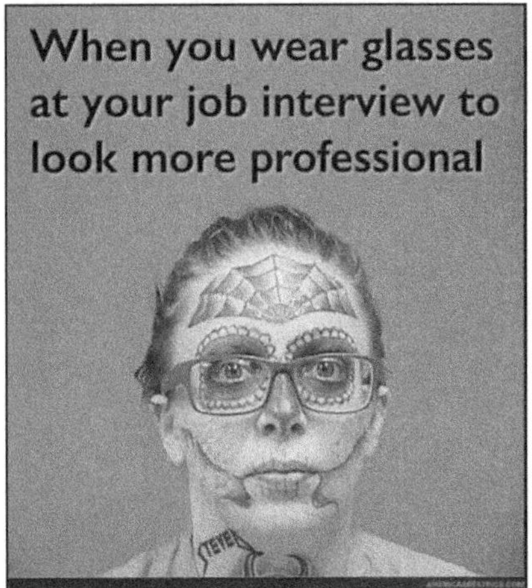

My favorite part of attending a marathon is watching the reaction of runners who grab my plastic cup of vodka.

Contributed by Tod Butler
10/27/2023

Software for All Problems

Dear Tech Support:

Last year I upgraded from Boyfriend 5.0 to Husband 1.0 and noticed a distinct slowdown in overall system performance, particularly in the flower and jewelry applications which had operated flawlessly under Boyfriend 5.0.

In addition, Husband 1.0 uninstalled many other valuable programs such as Romance 9.3 and Personal Attention 6.5 and then installed undesirable programs such as NBA 5.0 and Golf Clubs 4.1. Conversation 8.0 no longer runs, and House Cleaning 2.6 simply crashes the system. Please note that I have tried running Nagging 5.3 to fix the problems but to no avail. What can I do?

Signed,
Desperate

Dear Desperate:

First, keep in mind, Boyfriend 5.0 is an Entertainment Package while Husband 1.0 is an Operating System. Please enter the command: "I thought you loved me.html" and try to download Tears 6.2. Do not forget to install the Guilt 3.0 update. If that application works as designed, Husband 1.0 should then automatically run the applications Jewelry 2.0 and Flowers 3.5.

However, remember, overuse of the Tears application can cause Husband 1.0 to default to Grumpy Silence 2.5, Happy Hour 7.0, or Beer 6.1. Please not that Beer 6.1 is a very bad program that will download the Snoring Loudly Beta version.

Whatever you do, DO NOT, under any circumstances, install Mother-in-law 1.0 as it runs a virus in the background that will eventually seize control of all your system resources. In addition, please do not attempt to re-install Boyfriend 5.0 program. These are unsupported applications and will crash Husband 1.0.

In summary, Husband 1.0 is a great program, but it does have limited memory and cannot learn new applications quickly. You should consider buying additional software to improve memory and performance. We recommend Cooking 3.0.

Good Luck,
Tech Support

W.G. Williams
5/11/2024

Stealing McGlynn's Hat...

Murphy showed up at Mass one Sunday and the priest almost fell down when he saw him. Murphy had never been seen in church in his life.

After Mass, the priest caught Murphy and said, "Murphy, I am so glad you decided to come to Mass; what made you come?"

Murphy said, "I got to be honest with you, Father, a while back, I misplaced me hat and I really, really love that hat. I know that McGlynn had one just like mine and I knew that McGlynn came to church every Sunday.

"I also knew that McGlynn had to take off his hat during Mass and I figured he would leave it in the back of church. So, I was going to leave after Communion and steal McGlynn's hat."

The priest said, "Well Murphy, I notice that you didn't steal McGlynn's hat. What changed your mind?"

"Well, after I heard your sermon on the ten commandments, I decided that I didn't need to steal McGlynn's hat."

The priest gave Murphy a big smile and said, "After I talked about 'Thou Shalt Not Steal' you decided you would rather do without your hat than burn in Hell, right?"

Murphy shook his head and said, "No, Father; after you talked about 'Thou Shalt Not Commit Adultery' I remembered where I left me hat."

Contributed by Julius Graw
7/19/2005

Stop Illegal Immigration!

The flood of American liberals sneaking across the border into Canada has intensified in the past week, sparking calls for increased patrols to stop the illegal immigration. The actions of President Bush are prompting the exodus among left-leaning citizens who fear they'll soon be required to hunt, pray, and agree with Bill O'Reilly.

Canadian border farmers say it's not uncommon to see dozens of sociology professors, animal-rights activists and Unitarians crossing their fields at night.

"I went out to milk the cows the other day and there was a Hollywood producer huddled in the barn," said Manitoba farmer Red Greenfield, whose acreage borders North Dakota. "The producer was cold, exhausted and hungry. He asked me if I could spare a latte and some free-range chicken. When I said I didn't have any, he left. Didn't even get a chance to show him my screenplay, eh?"

In an effort to stop the illegal aliens, Greenfield erected higher fences, but the liberals scaled them. So he tried installing speakers that blare Rush Limbaugh across the fields. "Not real effective," he said. "The liberals still got through and Rush annoyed the cows so much they wouldn't give milk."

Officials are particularly concerned about smugglers who meet liberals near the Canadian border, pack them into Volvo station wagons, drive them across the border and leave them to fend for themselves.

"A lot of these people are not prepared for rugged conditions," an Ontario border patrolman said. "I found one carload without a drop of drinking water. "They did have a nice little Napa Valley cabernet, though."

When liberals are caught, they're sent back across the border, often wailing loudly that they fear retribution from conservatives. Rumors have been circulating about the Bush administration establishing re-education camps in which liberals will be forced to drink domestic beer and watch NASCAR races.

In recent days, liberals have turned to sometimes-ingenious ways of crossing the border. Some have taken to posing as senior citizens on bus trips to buy cheap Canadian prescription drugs.

After catching a half-dozen young vegans disguised in powdered wigs, Canadian immigration authorities began stopping buses and quizzing the supposed senior-citizen passengers on Perry Como and Rosemary Clooney hits to prove they were alive in the '50s. "If they can't identify the accordion player on The Lawrence Welk Show, we get suspicious about their age," an official said.

Canadian citizens have complained that the illegal immigrants are creating an organic-broccoli shortage and renting all the good Susan Sarandon movies. "I feel sorry for American liberals, but the Canadian economy just can't support them," an Ottawa resident said. "How many art-history majors does one country need?"

Contributed by Jim Phillips
1/25/2008

Stuff you didn't know you didn't know!

Men can read smaller print than women can; women can hear better.

Coca-Cola was originally green.

It is impossible to lick your elbow.

The state with the highest percentage of people who walk to work: Alaska

----

The percentage of Africa that is wilderness: 28% (now get this...)

The percentage of North America that is wilderness: 38%

The cost of raising a medium-size dog to the age of eleven: $16,400

The average number of people airborne over
the U.S. in any given hour: 61,000

Intelligent people have more zinc and copper in their hair.

The first novel ever written on a typewriter, <u>Tom Sawyer</u>.

The San Francisco Cable cars are the only mobile National Monuments.

Each king in a deck of playing cards represents a great king from history:
Spades - King David
Hearts - Charlemagne
Clubs -Alexander, the Great
Diamonds - Julius Caesar

111,111,111 x 111,111,111 = 12,345,678,987,654,321

If a statue in the park of a person on a horse has both front legs
in the air, the person died in battle.
If the horse has one front leg in the air, the person
died because of wounds received in battle.
If the horse has all four legs on the ground,
the person died of natural causes

Only two people signed the Declaration of Independence
on July 4, John Hancock and Charles Thomson. Most
of the rest signed on August 2, but the last
signature wasn't added until 5 years later.

Q. Half of all Americans live within 50 miles of what?
A. Their birthplace

Q. Most boat owners name their boats. What is
the most popular boat name requested?
A. Obsession

Q.. If you were to spell out numbers, how far would you
have to go until you would find the letter 'A'?
A. One thousand

Q. What do bulletproof vests, fire escapes, windshield wipers and
laser printers have in common?
A. All were invented by women.

Q. What is the only food that doesn't spoil?
A. Honey

Q. Which day are there more collect calls than any other day of the year?
A. Father's Day

In Shakespeare's time, mattresses were secured on bed frames
by ropes. When you pulled on the ropes, the mattress
tightened, making the bed firmer to sleep on.

Hence the phrase...'Goodnight, sleep tight.'

It was the accepted practice in Babylon 4,000 years ago that for a month after the wedding, the bride's father would supply his new son-in-law with all the mead he could drink. Mead is a honey beer and because their calendar was lunar based, this period was called the honey month, which we know today as the honeymoon.

In English pubs, ale is ordered by pints and quarts ... so in old England, when customers got unruly, the bartender would yell at them, 'Mind your pints and quarts, and settle down.'
It's where we get the phrase 'mind your P's and Q's.'

Many years ago in England, pub frequenters had a whistle baked into the rim, or handle, of their ceramic cups. When they needed a refill, they used the whistle to get some service.
'Wet your whistle' is the phrase inspired by this practice.

Probably 75% of the people who read this will try to lick their elbow!

YOU KNOW YOU ARE LIVING IN 2023 when...

1. You accidentally enter your PIN on the microwave.
2. You haven't played solitaire with real cards in years.
3. You have a list of 15 phone numbers to reach your family of three.
4. You e-mail the person who works at the desk next to you.
5. Your reason for not staying in touch with friends and family is that they don't have e-mail addresses.
6. You pull up in your own driveway and use your cell phone to see if anyone is home to help you carry in the groceries.
7. Every commercial on television has a Web site at the bottom of the screen
8. Leaving the house without your cell phone, which you didn't even have the first 20 or 30 (or 60) years of your life, is now a cause for panic and you turn around to go and get it!
10. You get up in the morning and go on-line before getting your coffee.
11. You start tilting your head sideways to smile. :)

12 You're reading this and nodding and laughing.
13. Even worse, you know exactly to whom you
are going to forward this message.
14. You are too busy to notice there was no #9 on this list.
15. You actually scrolled back up to check
that there wasn't a #9 on this list.

AND FINALLY
NOW you're LAUGHING at yourself!

Blessed are they who can laugh at themselves, for
they shall never cease to be amused!"
(Unknown Author)

Go on, forward this to your friends. You know you want to!
…And try to lick your elbow again!

Contributed by Ron Gargasz
6/2/2023

Stupid Court Comments...

* **Lawyer**: "Was that the same nose you broke as a child?"
* **Witness**: "I only have one, you know."

---

* **Lawyer**: "Now, Mrs. Johnson, how was your first marriage terminated?"
* **Witness**: "By death."
* **Lawyer**: "And by whose death was it terminated?"

---

* **Accused, Defending His Own Case**: "Did you get a good look at my face when I took your purse?"

The defendant was found guilty and sentenced to ten years in jail.

---

* **Lawyer**: "Can you tell us what was stolen from your house?"
* **Witness**: "There was a rifle that belonged to my father that was stolen from the hall closet."
* **Lawyer**: "Can you identify the rifle?"
* **Witness**: "Yes. There was something written on the side of it."
* **Lawyer**: "And what did the writing say?"
* **Witness**: "'Winchester'!"

---

* **Lawyer**: "Can you describe what the person who attacked you looked like?"
* **Witness**: "No. He was wearing a mask."
* **Lawyer**: "What was he wearing under the mask?"
* **Witness**: "Er…his face."

---

* **Lawyer**: "This myasthenia gravis — does it affect your memory at all?"
* **Witness**: "Yes."
* **Lawyer**: "And in what ways does it affect your memory?"
* **Witness**: "I forget."
* **Lawyer**: "You forget. Can you give us an example of something that you've forgotten?"

---

* **Lawyer**: "Sir, what is your IQ?"
* **Witness**: "Well, I can see pretty well, I think."

---

* **Lawyer**: "Did you blow your horn or anything?"
* **Witness**: "After the accident?"
* **Lawyer**: "Before the accident."
* **Witness**: "Sure, I played for ten years. I even went to school for it."

---

* **Lawyer**: "Trooper, when you stopped the defendant, were your red and blue lights flashing?"
* **Witness**: "Yes."
* **Lawyer**: "Did the defendant say anything when she got out of her car?"
* **Witness**: "Yes, sir."
* **Lawyer**: "What did she say?"
* **Witness**: "'What disco am I at?'"

---

* **Lawyer**: "How far apart were the vehicles at the time of the collision?"

---

* **Lawyer**: "And you check your radar unit frequently?"
* **Officer**: "Yes, I do."

* **Lawyer**: "And was your radar unit functioning correctly at the time you had the plaintiff on radar?"
* **Officer**: "Yes, it was malfunctioning correctly."

---

* **Lawyer**: "What happened then?"
* **Witness**: "He told me, he says, 'I have to kill you because you can identify me.'"
* **Lawyer**: "Did he kill you?"
* **Witness**: "No."

---

* **Lawyer**: "Now sir, I'm sure you are an intelligent and honest man–"
* **Witness**: "Thank you. If I weren't under oath, I'd return the compliment."

---

* **Lawyer**: "You were there until the time you left, is that true?"

---

* **Lawyer**: "So you were gone until you returned?"

---

* **Lawyer**: "The youngest son, the 20-year-old, how old is he?"

---

* **Lawyer**: "Were you alone or by yourself?"

---

* **Lawyer**: "How long have you been a French Canadian?"

---

* **Witness**: "He was about medium height and had a beard."
* **Lawyer**: "Was this a male or a female?"

---

* **Lawyer**: "Mr. Slatery, you went on a rather elaborate honeymoon, didn't you?"
* **Witness**: "I went to Europe, sir."
* **Lawyer**: "And you took your new wife?"

---

* **Lawyer**: "I show you Exhibit 3 and ask you if you recognize that picture."
* **Witness**: "That's me."
* **Lawyer**: "Were you present when that picture was taken?"

---

* **Lawyer**: "Were you present in court this morning when you were sworn in?"

---

* **Lawyer**: "Do you know how far pregnant you are now?"
* **Witness**: "I'll be three months on November 8."
* **Lawyer**: "Apparently, then, the date of conception was August 8?"
* **Witness**: "Yes."
* **Lawyer**: "What were you doing at that time?"

---

* **Lawyer**: "How many times have you committed suicide?"
* **Witness**: "Four times."

---

* **Lawyer**: "Do you have any children or anything of that kind?"

---

* **Lawyer**: "You don't know what it was, and you didn't know what it looked like, but can you describe it?"

---

* **Lawyer**: "You say that the stairs went down to the basement?"
* **Witness**: "Yes."
* **Lawyer**: "And these stairs, did they go up also?"

---

* **Lawyer**: "Have you lived in this town all your life?"
* **Witness**: "Not yet."

---

* **Lawyer**: (realizing he was on the verge of asking a stupid question) "Your Honor, I'd like to strike the next question."

---

* **Lawyer**: "Do you recall approximately the time that you examined the body of Mr. Eddington at the Rose Chapel?"
* **Witness**: "It was in the evening. The autopsy started about 8:30pm."
* **Lawyer**: "And Mr. Eddington was dead at the time, is that correct?"

---

* **Lawyer**: "What is your brother-in-law's name?"
* **Witness**: "Borofkin."
* **Lawyer**: "What's his first name?"
* **Witness**: "I can't remember."
* **Lawyer**: "He's been your brother-in-law for years, and you can't remember his first name?"
* **Witness**: "No. I tell you, I'm too excited." (rising and pointing to his brother-in-law) "Nathan, for heaven's sake, tell them your first name!"

---

* **Lawyer**: "Did you ever stay all night with this man in New York?"
* **Witness**: "I refuse to answer that question.
* **Lawyer**: "Did you ever stay all night with this man in Chicago?"
* **Witness**: "I refuse to answer that question.
* **Lawyer**: "Did you ever stay all night with this man in Miami?"
* **Witness**: "No."

---

* **Lawyer**: "Doctor, did you say he was shot in the woods?"
* **Witness**: "No, I said he was shot in the lumbar region."

---

* **Lawyer**: "What is your marital status?"
* **Witness**: "Fair."

---

* **Lawyer**: "Are you married?"
* **Witness**: "No, I'm divorced."
* **Lawyer**: "And what did your husband do before you divorced him?"
* **Witness**: "A lot of things I didn't know about."

---

* **Lawyer**: "And who is this person you are speaking of?"
* **Witness**: "My ex-widow said it.

---

* **Lawyer**: "How did you happen to go to Dr. Cherney?"
* **Witness**: "Well, a gal down the road had had several of her children by Dr. Cherney and said he was really good."

---

* **Lawyer**: "Were you acquainted with the deceased?"
* **Witness**: "Yes sir."
* **Lawyer**: "Before or after he died?"

---

* **Lawyer**: "Mrs. Jones, is your appearance this morning pursuant to a deposition notice which I sent to your attorney?"
* **Witness**: "No. This is how I dress when I go to work."

---

* **The Court**: "Now, as we begin, I must ask you to banish all present information and prejudice from your minds, if you have any."

---

* **Lawyer**: "Did he pick the dog up by the ears?"
* **Witness**: "No."
* **Lawyer**: "What was he doing with the dog's ears?"
* **Witness**: "Picking them up in the air."
* **Lawyer**: "Where was the dog at this time?"
* **Witness**: "Attached to the ears."

---

* **Lawyer**: "When he went, had you gone and had she, if she wanted to and were able, for the time being excluding all the restraints on her not to go, gone also, would he have brought you, meaning you and she, with him to the station?"
* **Other Lawyer**: "Objection. That question should be taken out and shot."

---

* **Lawyer**: "And lastly, Gary, all your responses must be oral. Ok? What school do you go to?"
* **Witness**: "Oral."
* **Lawyer**: "How old are you?"
* **Witness**: "Oral."

---

* **Lawyer**: "What is your relationship with the plaintiff?"
* **Witness**: "She is my daughter."
* **Lawyer**: "Was she your daughter on February 13, 1979?"

---

* **Lawyer**: "Now, you have investigated other murders, have you not, where there was a victim?"

---

* **Lawyer**: "Now, doctor, isn't it true that when a person dies in his sleep, in most cases he just passes quietly away and doesn't know anything about it until the next morning?"

---

* **Lawyer**: "And what did he do then?"
* **Witness**: "He came home, and next morning he was dead."
* **Lawyer**: "So when he woke up the next morning he was dead?"

---

* **Lawyer**: "Did you tell your lawyer that your husband had offered you indignities?"
* **Witness**: "He didn't offer me nothing. He just said I could have the furniture."

---

* **Lawyer**: "So, after the anesthesia, when you came out of it, what did you observe with respect to your scalp?"
* **Witness**: "I didn't see my scalp the whole time I was in the hospital."
* **Lawyer**: "It was covered?"
* **Witness**: "Yes, bandaged."
* **Lawyer**: "Then, later on…what did you see?"
* **Witness**: "I had a skin graft. My whole buttocks and leg were removed and put on top of my head."

---

* **Lawyer**: "Could you see him from where you were standing?"
* **Witness**: "I could see his head."
* **Lawyer**: "And where was his head?"
* **Witness**: "Just above his shoulders."

---

* **Lawyer**: "Do you drink when you're on duty?"
* **Witness**: "I don't drink when I'm on duty, unless I come on duty drunk."

---

* **Lawyer**: "Any suggestions as to what prevented this from being a murder trial instead of an attempted murder trial?"

*   **Witness**: "The victim lived."

---

*   **Lawyer**: "The truth of the matter is that you were not an unbiased, objective witness, isn't it? You too were shot in the fracas."
*   **Witness**: "No, sir. I was shot midway between the fracas and the naval."

---

*   **Lawyer**: "Officer, what led you to believe the defendant was under the influence?"
*   **Witness**: "Because he was argumentary, and he couldn't pronunciate his words."

Contributed by David A. Silverman
1/7/2010

Tales of the Not-So-Smart...

1. When his 38 caliber revolver failed to fire at his intended victim during a hold-up in Long Beach, California, would-be robber James Elliot did something that can only inspire wonder. He peered down the barrel and tried the trigger again. This time it worked.

2. The chef at a hotel in Switzerland lost a finger in a meat cutting machine and after a little shopping around, submitted a claim to his insurance company. The company expecting negligence sent out one of its men to have a look for himself. He tried the machine and he also lost a finger.. The chef's claim was approved.

3. A man who shoveled snow for an hour to clear a space for his car during a blizzard in Chicago returned with his vehicle to find a woman had taken the space. Understandably, he shot her.

4. After stopping for drinks at an illegal bar, a Zimbabwean bus driver found that the 20 mental patients he was supposed to be transporting from Harare to Bulawayo had escaped. Not wanting to admit his incompetence, the driver went to a nearby bus stop and offered everyone waiting there a free ride. He then delivered the passengers to the mental hospital, telling the staff that the patients were very excitable and prone to bizarre fantasies. The deception wasn't discovered for three days.

5. An American teenager was in the hospital recovering from serious head wounds received from an oncoming train. When asked how he received the injuries, the lad told police that he was simply trying to see how close he could get his head to a moving train before he was hit.

6. A man walked into a Louisiana Circle-K, put a $20 bill on the counter, and asked for change. When the clerk opened the cash drawer, the man pulled a gun and asked for all the cash in the register, which the clerk promptly provided. The man took the cash from the clerk and fled, leaving the $20 bill on the counter. The total amount of cash he got from the drawer... $15. [If someone points a gun at you and gives you money, is a crime committed?]

7. Seems an Arkansas guy wanted some beer pretty badly. He decided that he'd just throw a cinder block through a liquor store window, grab some booze, and run. So he lifted the cinder block and heaved it over his head at the window. The cinder block bounced back and hit the would-be thief on the head, knocking him unconscious. The liquor store window was made of Plexiglas. The whole event was caught on videotape...

8. As a female shopper exited a New York convenience store, a man grabbed her purse and ran. The clerk called 911 immediately and the woman was able to give them a detailed description of the snatcher. Within minutes, the police apprehended the snatcher. They put him in the car and drove back to the store. The thief was then taken out of the car and told to stand there for a positive ID. To which he replied, "Yes, officer, that's her. That's the lady I stole the purse from."

9. The Ann Arbor News crime column reported that a man walked into a Burger King in Ypsilanti, Michigan at 5 A.M., flashed a gun, and demanded cash. The clerk turned him down because he said he couldn't open the cash register without a food order. When the man ordered onion rings, the clerk said they weren't available for breakfast. The man, frustrated, walked away.

10. When a man attempted to siphon gasoline from a motor home parked on a Seattle street by sucking on a hose, he got much more than he bargained for. Police arrived at the scene to find a very sick man curled up next to a motor home near spilled sewage. A police spokesman said that the man admitted to trying to steal gasoline, but he plugged his siphon hose into the motor home's sewage tank by mistake. The

owner of the vehicle declined to press charges saying that it was the best laugh he'd ever had.

In the interest of bettering mankind, please share these with friends and family unless, of course, one of these individuals by chance is a distant relative or long lost friend. In that case, be glad they are distant and hope they remain lost.

Remember... They VOTE!

Contributed by Sharon Buckholtz
9/5/2022

Tampons to the Rescue in Iraq!

(Don't worry, it's a good story from the mother of a Marine in Iraq.)

My son told me how wonderful the care packages we had sent them were and wanted me to tell everyone, "Thank you." He said that one guy, we'll call him Marine X, got a girl's care package and everyone was giving him a hard time. My son said, "Marine X got some really nice smelling lotion and everyone really likes it, so every time he goes to sleep they steal it from him."

I told my son I was really sorry about the mistake and, if he wanted, I would send Marine X another package.

He told me not to worry about Marine X because every time I send something to my son, Marine X thinks it's for him too. He said when my husband and I sent the last care package, Marine X came over to his cot picked up the box, started fishing through it, and said, "What'd we get this time?"

My son said they had the most fun with Marine X's package. He said he wasn't sure who we were sending the pack to, but the panties were size 20. He said one of the guys got on top of the Humvee and jumped off with the panties over his head and yelled, "Look at me, I'm an Airborne Ranger!" Later, one of the guys attached the panties to an antenna and it blew in the wind like a windsock. He said it entertained them for quite a while.

Then of course, they had the tampons.

When he brought this up, my imagination just went running, but he continued. My son said they had to go on a mission and Marine X wanted the ChapStick and lotion for the trip. He grabbed a bunch of items from his care package and got in the Humvee. As luck would have it he grabbed the tampons too, and my son said everyone was teasing him about "not forgetting his feminine hygiene products."

He said things went well for a while, then the convoy was ambushed, and a Marine was shot. He said the wound was pretty clean, but it was deep. He said they were administering first aid but couldn't get the bleeding to slow down, and someone said, "Hey use Marine X's tampons."

My son said they put the tampon in the wound. At this point my son profoundly told me, "Mom did you know that tampons expand?"

"Well, yeah!"

They successfully slowed the bleeding until the guy got better medical attention. When they went to check on him later the surgeon told them, "You guys saved his life. If you hadn't stopped that bleeding, he would have bled to death."

My son said, "Mom, the tampons sent by the Marine Moms by mistake saved a Marine's life."

At this point I asked him, "Well what did you do with the rest of the tampons?"

He said, "Oh, we divided them up and we all have them in our flak jackets, and I kept two for our first aid kit."

I am absolutely amazed by the ingenuity of our Marines and can't believe that something that started out as a mistake then turned into a joke, ended up saving someone's life. My sister said she doesn't believe in mistakes. She believes God had a plan all along. She believes that female care package was sent to Marine X to save his buddy

Either way ladies, our efforts have boosted the morale of many Marines, provided much needed items for our troops, AND saved the life of a Marine! God bless every one of you for your efforts and hard work, and God bless our Marines, Army, Navy, Air Force, and everyone.

Contributed by Bubba & Bonnie Mehling
11/25/2006

Tenjewberrymuds

The following is a telephone exchange between a hotel guest and room-service at a hotel in Asia, which was recorded and published in the *Far East Economic Review:*

Room Service (RS): "Morrin. Roon sirbees."
Guest (G): "Sorry, I thought I dialed room-service."
RS: "Rye..Roon sirbees..morrin! Jewish to oddor sunteen??"
G: "Uh..yes..I'd like some bacon and eggs."
RS: "Ow July den?"
G: "What??"
RS: "Ow July den?...pryed, boyud, poochd?"
G: "Oh, the eggs! How do I like them? Sorry, scrambled please."
RS: "Ow July dee baykem? Crease?"
G: "Crisp will be fine."
RS: "Hokay. An Sahn toes?"
G: "What?"
RS: "An toes. July Sahn toes?"
G: "I don't think so."
RS: "No? Judo wan sahn toes??"
G: "I feel really bad about this, but I don't know what 'judo wan sahn toes' means."
RS: "Toes! toes!...Why jew don juan toes? Ow bow Anglish moppin we bodder?"
G: "English muffin!! I've got it! You were saying 'Toast.' Fine. Yes, an English muffin will be fine."
RS: "We bodder?"
G: "No...just put the bodder on the side."
RS: "Wad?"
G: "I mean butter...just put it on the side."
RS: "Copy?"

G: "Excuse me?"
RS: "Copy...tea...meel?"
G: "Yes. Coffee, please, and that's all."
RS: "One Minnie. Scramah egg, crease bay kem, Anglish moppin we bodder on sigh and copy....rye??"
G: "Whatever you say."
RS: "Tenjewberrymuds."
G: "You're very welcome."

Contributed by Ron Heisler
9/12/2005

That's How We Drink

A cowboy, who just moved to Montana from Texas, walked into a bar and ordered three mugs of Bud. He sat in the back of the room and drank a sip out of each one in turn.

When he finished them, he came back to the bar and ordered three more.

The bartender approached and said, "You know, a mug goes flat after I draw it. It would taste better if you bought one at a time."

The cowboy replied, "I know, but you see, I have two brothers. One is in Arizona; the other is in Colorado. When we all left our home in Texas, we promised that we'd drink this way to remember the days when we drank together. So, I'm drinking one beer for each of my brothers and one for myself."

The bartender admitted that this seemed like a nice custom and left it there.

The cowboy became a regular in the bar and always drank the same way. He would order three mugs and drink them in turn.

One day, he came in and only ordered two mugs. All the regulars took notice and fell silent.

When he went back to the bar for the second round, the bartender said, "I don't want to intrude on your grief, but I wanted to offer my condolences on your loss."

The cowboy looked quite puzzled for a moment, then a light dawned in his eyes, and he laughed. "Oh, no, everybody's just fine," he explained. "It's just that my wife and I joined the Baptist Church and I had to quit drinking."

Contributed by Mark Hopkins
1/15/2024

The AFLAC Scam

Watch out for this scam. Police say that the gang usually is comprised of four members, one adult and three younger ones.

While the three younger ones, all appearing sweet and innocent, divert their 'mark' (or intended target) with a show of friendliness, the fourth -- the eldest -- sneaks in from behind the person's back to expertly rifle through his or her pockets and purses or bags for any valuables being carried.

The attached picture shows the gang in operation.

Contributed by David Taylor
4/2/2008

The Bible (According to Kids!)

The following statements about the bible were written by elementary school children. They have not been retouched or corrected (i.e., incorrect spelling has been left in).

1. In the first book of the bible, Guinessis, God got tired of creating the world, so he took the Sabbath off.

2. Adam and Eve were created from an apple tree. Noah's wife was called Joan of Ark. Noah built an ark which the animals come on to in pears.

3. Lot's wife was a pillar of salt by day, but a ball of fire by night.

4. The Jews were a proud people and throughout history they had trouble with the unsympathetic Genitals.

5. Samson was a strongman who let himself be led astray by a Jezebel like Delilah.

6. Samson slayed the Philistines with the axe of the Apostles.

7. Moses led the hebrews to the Red Sea, where they made unleavened bread which is bread without any ingredients.

8. The Egyptians were all drowned in the dessert. Afterwards, Moses went up on Mount Cyanide to get the ten ammendments.

9. The first commandment was when Eve told Adam to eat the apple.

10. The seventh commandment is thou shalt not admit adultery.

11. Moses died before he ever reached Canada. Then Joshua led the Hebrews in the battle of Geritol.

12. The greatest miracle in the Bible is when Joshua told his son to stand still and he obeyed him.

13. David was a Hebrew king skilled at playing the liar. He fought with the Finklesteins, a race of people who lived in Biblical times.

14. Solomon, one of David's sons, had 300 wives and 700 porcupines.

15. When Mary heard that she was the mother of Jesus, she sang the Magna Carta.

16. When the three wise guys from the east side arrived, they found Jesus in the manager.

17. Jesus was born because Mary had an immaculate contraption.

18. St. John the blacksmith dumped water on his head.

19. Jesus enunciated the Golden Rule, which says to do one to others before they do one to you. He also explained, "a man doth not live by sweat alone."

20. It was a miracle when Jesus rose from the dead and managed to get the tombstone off the entrance.

21. The people who followed the lord were called the 12 decibels.

22. The epistles were the wives of the apostles.

23. One of the oppossums was St. Matthew who was also a taximan.

24. St. Paul cavorted to Christianity. He preached holy acrimony, which is another name for marriage.

25. Christians have only one spouse. This is called monotony.

Contributed by David Taylor
10/13/2009

The Bus Ride...

Two bowling teams, one of all Blondes and one of all Brunettes, chartered a double-Decker bus for a weekend trip. The Brunette team rode on the bottom of the bus and the Blonde team rode on the top level.

The Brunette team down below was really whooping it up and having a great time when one of them realized that she hadn't heard anything from the Blondes upstairs. She decided to go up and investigate.

When she reached the top, she found all the Blondes in fear, staring straight ahead at the road, clutching the seats in front of them with white knuckles. The brunette asked, "What the heck's going on up here? We're having a great time downstairs!"

One of the Blondes looked up at her, swallowed hard and replied, "YEAH, BUT YOU'VE GOT A DRIVER!"

Contributed by David Taylor
3/6/2009

The Cab Ride

A cabbie picked up a nun. She got into the cab and noticed that the very handsome cab driver wouldn't stop staring at her. She asked him why he was staring, and he replied: "I have a question to ask you, but I don't want to offend you."

She answered, "My son, you can't offend me. When you're as old as I am and have been a nun as long as I have, you get a chance to see and hear just about everything. I'm sure that there's nothing you could say or ask that I would find offensive."

"Well, I've always had a fantasy to have a nun kiss me."

She responded, "Well, let's see what we can do about that: #1, you have to be single and #2, you must be Catholic."

The cab driver became very excited and said, "Yes, I'm single and Catholic!"

"OK" the nun replied. "Pull into the next alley."

There the nun fulfilled the cab driver's fantasy with a kiss that would make a hooker blush. But when they got back on the road, the cab driver started crying.

"My dear child," said the nun, "why are you crying?"

"Forgive me but I have sinned. I lied and I must confess, I'm married and I'm Jewish."

The nun said, "That's OK. My name is Kevin and I'm going to a Halloween party."

Contributed by Misty Ankney
10/25/2005

The Cow from Maine

Ted and Bob did some research and found they could buy a cow in Maine for $200.00. Since that was a great price, they went to Maine and bought the cow. When they got back, they realized that the cow was wonderful. It produced lots of milk all of the time and they were pleased and very happy.

They then decided to acquire a bull to mate with the cow and produce more cows like it. If they were successful, they'd never have to worry about their milk supply again.

On their next trip to Maine, they bought a bull and put it in the pasture with their beloved cow. However, whenever the bull came close to the cow, the cow would move away. No matter what approach the bull tried, the cow would move away, and the bull could not succeed in his quest.

Ted and Bob were very upset and decided to ask their veterinarian what to do.

They told the Vet what was happening. "Whenever the bull approaches our cow, she moves away. If he approaches from the back, she moves forward. When he approaches her from the front, she backs off. An approach from the side and she walks away to the other side."

The Vet thought about this for a minute and asked, "Did you buy this cow in Maine?"

Ted and Bob were dumbfounded since they had never mentioned where they bought the cow. "Boy! You really know your stuff," Ted said. "How did you know we got the cow in Maine?

The Vet replied with a distant look in his eye, "My wife is from Maine..."

Contributed by Ron Gargasz
8/8/2012

The Dangers of Bread!

A recent newspaper headline read, "Smell of baked bread may be health hazard." The article described the dangers associated with the smell of baking bread. The main danger, apparently, is that the organic components of this aroma may break down ozone.

When are we going to do something about bread-induced global warming? Sure, we attack tobacco companies but when is the government going to go after Big Bread? A little research reveals some startling facts, which should make anyone, think twice:

- More than 98 percent of convicted felons are bread eaters.
- Fully HALF of all children who grow up in bread-consuming households score below average on standardized tests.
- In the 18th century, when virtually all bread was baked in the home, the average life expectancy was less than 50 years; infant mortality rates were unacceptably high; many women died in childbirth; and diseases such as typhoid, yellow fever and influenza ravaged whole nations.
- More than 90 percent of violent crimes are committed within 24 hours of eating bread.
- Bread is made from a substance called dough. It has been proven that as little as one pound of dough can be used to suffocate a mouse. The average American eats more bread than that in one month.
- Primitive tribal societies that have no bread exhibit a low occurrence of cancer, Alzheimer`s, Parkinson`s disease and osteoporosis.
- Bread has been proven to be addictive. Subjects deprived of bread and given only water to eat begged for bread after only two days.
- Bread is often a "gateway" food item, leading the user to "harder" items such as butter, jelly, peanut butter and even cold cuts.
- Bread has been proven to absorb water. Since the human body is more than 90 percent water, it follows that eating bread could

lead to your body being taken over by this absorptive food product, turning you into a soggy, gooey bread-pudding person.
- Newborn babies can choke on bread.
- Bread is baked at temperatures as high as 400 F. That kind of heat can kill an adult in less than one minute.
- Most American bread eaters are utterly unable to distinguish between significant scientific fact and meaningless statistical babbling.

In light of these frightening statistics, concerned citizens have proposed the following bread restrictions:
- No sale of bread to minors;
- No advertising of bread within 1,000 feet of a school;
- A 300 percent federal tax on all bread to pay for the societal ills associated with bread;
- No animal or human images, nor any primary colors (which may appeal to children) may be used to promote bread usage; and
- A $4.2 billion fine on the three biggest bread manufacturers.

We must fight this danger NOW!

Contributed by Bonnie & Bubba Mehling
10/8/2005

The Deaf Bookkeeper

A Mafia Godfather found out that his bookkeeper, Guido, had cheated him out of $10,000,000.00.

His bookkeeper was deaf; that was the reason he got the job in the first place. It was assumed that Guido would hear nothing and would therefore never have to testify in court.

When the Godfather confronted Guido about the missing $10 million, he took along his lawyer, who knew sign language. The Godfather told the lawyer, "Ask him where the money is."

The lawyer, using sign language, asked Guido, "Where's the money?"

Guido signed back, "I don't know what you're talking about."

The lawyer told the Godfather, "He says he doesn't know what you're talking about."

The Godfather pulled out a pistol, put it to Guido's head and said, "Ask him again or I'll kill him!"

The lawyer signed to Guido, "He'll kill you if you don't tell him."

Guido trembled and signed back, "OK! You win! The money is in a brown brief case buried behind the shed at my cousin Bruno's house."

The Godfather asked the lawyer, "What did he say?"

The lawyer replied, "He said you don't have the guts to pull the trigger."

(Don't you just love lawyers?)

Contributed by Ron Heisler
7/1/12019

The Drug Problem in America...

The other day, someone at a store in our town read that a methamphetamine lab had been found in an old farmhouse in the adjoining county and he asked me a rhetorical question, "Why didn't we have a drug problem when you and I were growing up?"

I replied, "I had a drug problem when I was young:

"I was drug to church on Sunday morning.

"I was drug to church for weddings and funerals.

"I was drug to family reunions and community socials no matter the weather.

"I was drug by my ears when I was disrespectful to adults.

"I was also drug to the woodshed when I disobeyed my parents, told a lie, brought home a bad report card, did not speak with respect, spoke ill of the teacher or the preacher, or if I didn't put forth my best effort in everything that was asked of me.

"I was drug to the kitchen sink to have my mouth washed out with soap if I uttered a profane four-letter word.

"I was drug out to pull weeds in mom's garden and flower beds and cockleburs out of dad's fields.

"I was drug to the homes of family, friends, and neighbors to help out some poor soul who had no one to mow the yard, repair the clothesline, or chop some firewood; and, if my mother had ever known that I took a single dime as a tip for this kindness, she would have drug me back to the woodshed."

Those drugs are still in my veins; and they affect my behavior in everything I do, say, and think. They are stronger than cocaine, crack, or heroin; and, if today's children had this kind of drug problem, America would be a better place.

Contributed by Misty Ankney
2/23/2006

The Fix

Some time ago an article appeared in the <u>St. Petersburg Times </u>in Florida. The Business Section had asked readers for ideas on: "How Would You Fix the Economy?"
I think this guy nailed it!

Dear Mr. President, Please find below my
suggestion for fixing America 's economy:
Instead of giving billions of dollars to companies that
will squander the money on lavish parties and unearned
bonuses, use the following plan. You can call it:

"The Patriotic Retirement Plan"

There are about 40 million people over 50 in the work
force. Pay them $1 million apiece severance for early
retirement with the following stipulations:

1) They MUST retire. Forty million job openings = Unemployment fixed.

2) They MUST buy a new AMERICAN Car. Forty
million cars ordered = Auto Industry fixed.

3) They MUST either buy a house or pay off
their mortgage = Housing Crisis fixed.

It can't get any easier than that!!

P.S. If more money is needed, have all members
in Congress pay their taxes.

Mr. President, while you're at it, make Congress retire on Social
Security and Medicare. I'll bet both programs would be fixed pronto!

Contributed by Ron Gargasz
9/21/2013

The Golf Nut...

Ed and Nancy met while on a singles cruise and Ed fell head over heels for her. When they discovered they lived in the same city only a few miles apart Ed was ecstatic. He immediately started asking her out when they got home.

Within a couple of weeks, Ed had taken Nancy to dance clubs, restaurants, concerts, movies, and museums. Ed became convinced that Nancy was indeed his soul mate and true love. Every date seemed better than the last.

On the one-month anniversary of their first dinner on the cruise ship, Ed took Nancy to a fine restaurant. While having cocktails and waiting for their salad, Ed said, "I guess you can tell I'm very much in love with you. I'd like a little serious talk before our relationship continues to the next stage.

"So, before I get a box out of my jacket and ask you a life changing question, it's only fair to warn you, I'm a total golf nut. I play golf, I read about golf, I watch golf on TV. In short, I eat, sleep, and breathe golf. If that's going to be a problem for us, you'd better say so now!"

Nancy took a deep breath and responded, "Ed, that certainly won't be a problem. I love you as you are and I love golf too; but, since we're being totally honest with each other, you need to know that for the last five years I've been a hooker."

"Oh wow! I see," Ed replied. He looked down at the table, was quiet for a moment. Deep in serious thought then he added, "You know, it's probably because you're not keeping your wrists straight when you hit the ball."

Contributed by Ron Gargasz
01-01-2011

The Indians' Point of View...

An old Indian chief sat in his hut on the reservation, smoking a ceremonial pipe and eyeing two US government officials sent to interview him.

"Chief Two Eagles," asked one official, "You have observed the white man for 90 years. You've seen his wars and his material wealth. You've seen his progress, and the damage he's done."

The chief nodded that it was so.

The official continued, "Considering all these events, in your opinion, where did the white man go wrong?"

The chief stared at the government officials for over a minute and then calmly replied, "When the white man found the land, the Indians were running it. We had no taxes, no debt, no borders, plenty of buffalo and beaver, the women did all the work, the medicine man was free, and Indian men spent all day hunting and fishing and all-night having sex."

Then the chief leaned back and smiled, "The problem is that the white man was dumb enough to think he could improve a system like that!"

Contributed by Gary Thornton
8/25/2006

The Lamaze Class...

The room was full of pregnant women, with their partners. The Lamaze class was in full swing. The instructor was teaching the women how to breathe properly and was telling the men how to give the necessary assurances to their partners at this stage of the pregnancy.

She said, "Ladies, remember that exercise is GOOD for you. Walking is especially beneficial. It strengthens the pelvic muscles and will make delivery that much easier!"

She looked at the men in the room. "And gentlemen, remember, you're in this together. So it wouldn't hurt you to go walking with your partner."

The room suddenly got very quiet as the men absorbed this information. Then a man at the back of the room slowly raised his hand.

"Yes?" asked the teacher.

"I was just wondering," the man said. "Is it all right if she carries a golf bag while we walk?"

Contributed by Gary Thornton
10/5/2006

The Monk...

A man was driving down a country road when his car broke down near a monastery. He went to the monastery, knocked on the door, and said, "My car broke down. Do you think I could stay the night?"

The monks graciously accepted him, fed him dinner, and even fixed his car. As the man tried to fall asleep, he heard a strange sound…a sound not like anything he'd ever heard before. The Sirens that nearly seduced Odysseus into crashing his ship came into his mind.

He didn't sleep that night. He tossed and turned trying to figure out what could possibly be making such a seductive sound. The next morning, he asked the monks what the sound was, but they claimed, "We can't tell you. You're not a monk."

Distraught, the man was forced to leave. Years later, after never being able to forget that sound, he went back to the monastery and pled again for the answer.

Again the monks replied, "We can't tell you. You're not a monk."

"If the only way I can find out what is making that beautiful sound is to become a monk, then please, allow me to become a monk."

In reply he heard, "You must travel the earth and tell us how many blades of grass there are and the exact number of grains of sand. When you find these answers, you will have become a monk."

The man set about his task. After years of searching, he returned and knocked again on the door of the monastery. "I have traveled the earth and have found what you have asked: By design, the world is in a state of perpetual change. Only God knows what you ask. All a man can know is himself, and then only if he is honest and reflective and willing to strip away self-deception."

The monks replied, "Congratulations. You are now a monk. We shall now show you the way to the mystery of the sound."

The monks led the man to a wooden door, where the abbot said, "The sound is beyond that door." Then they gave him the key.

When he opened the door, he found another door, this one made of stone. He was then given the key to the stone door. When he opened it, he found a door made of ruby. And so it went that he needed keys to doors of emerald, gold and diamond.

Finally, the monks said, "This is the last key to the last door."

The man was tremendously apprehensive; his life's wish was behind the door! He unlocked the door, turned the knob, and behind that door he was utterly amazed to find that the source of that haunting and seductive sound was...

...But I can't tell you what it was because you're not a monk.

Contributed by David Taylor
June 7, 2006

The Old "Light Bulb" Joke...

How many members of the Bush Administration are needed to change a light bulb? The Answer is TEN:

1. One to deny that the light bulb needs to be changed,

2. One to attack the patriotism of anyone who says the light bulb needs to be changed,

3. One to blame Clinton for burning out the light bulb,

4. One to tell the nations of the world that they are either for changing the light bulb or for darkness

5. One to give a billion dollar no-bid contract to Halliburton for the new light bulb,

6. One to arrange a photograph of Bush, dressed as a janitor, standing on a step ladder under the banner -- Light bulb Change Accomplished,

7. One administration insider to resign and write a book documenting in detail how Bush was literally in the dark,

8. One to viciously smear #7,

9. One surrogate to campaign on TV and at rallies on how George Bush has had a strong light-bulb changing policy all along, and

10. Finally, one to confuse Americans about the difference between screwing a light bulb and screwing the country.

Contributed by Ron Gargasz
8/23/2006

The Pope's Alaskan Tour...

On a tour of Alaska, the Pope took a couple of days off to visit the mountains for some sightseeing. He was cruising along in the Pope-mobile when there was a frantic commotion at the edge of the woods. A Democrat was struggling frantically, thrashing around trying to free himself from the jaws of a 10-foot grizzly.

As the Pope watched horrified, a group of Republicans came racing up. One quickly fired a .44 magnum into the bear's chest. The other two reached up and pulled the bleeding semiconscious Democrat from the bear. Then using long clubs, the three Republicans beat the bear to death and two of them threw it onto the bed of their truck while the other tenderly placed the injured Democrat in the back seat.

As they prepared to leave, the Pope summoned them to come over. "I give you my blessing for your brave actions!" he told them. "I heard there was a bitter hatred between Republicans and Democrats, but now I've seen with my own eyes that is not true."

As the Pope drove off, one of the Republicans asked his buddies "Who was that guy?"

"It was the Pope," another replied, "he's in direct contact with God and has access to all God's wisdom."

"Well," the Republican said, "he may have access to all God's wisdom, but he sure doesn't know anything about bear hunting. By the way, is the bait holding up okay or do we need to go back to town and grab another one?"

Contributed by Gary Thornton
12/8/2005

The Poverty of Words...

The teacher said to his disciples, "Those who know, do not say and those who say, do not know."

The confused disciples inquired as to the meaning of this saying.
The teacher said, "How many know the smell of a rose?"
All nodded.
"Put it into words," he said.
And all remained silent.

Contributed by Chris Clody
5/14/2010

The Power of Words...

Once upon a time a group of guys arranged a competition. The goal was to reach the top of a very high tower.

A big crowd had gathered around the tower to see the race and cheer on the contestants.

The race began....

Honestly, no one in the crowd really believed that the contestants would reach the top of the tower. You heard statements such as:

"Oh, it's WAY too difficult!"

"They'll NEVER make it to the top."

or:

"There's not a chance that they will succeed. The tower's too high!"

The climbers began collapsing. One by one.... except for those, who in a fresh effort, were climbing higher and higher.

The crowd continued to yell, "It's too difficult!!! No one will make it!"

More got tired and gave up...but ONE continued higher and higher and higher. This one wouldn't give up!

At the end everyone else had given up climbing the tower...except for the one who, after a big effort, was the only one who reached the top!

THEN all of the others naturally wanted to know how this one small boy managed to do it? One of the others asked him how he had found the strength! to succeed and reach the goal?

It turned out that the winner was DEAF!!!

The wisdom of this story is this:

Never listen to other people's tendencies to be negative or pessimistic because they take your most wonderful dreams and wishes away from you -- the ones you have in your heart!

Always think of the power words have because everything you hear and read will affect your actions!

Therefore ALWAYS be POSITIVE! And above all, be DEAF when people tell YOU that you can't succeed! Always think -- I CAN do this!

Remember the words of the great prophet Yoda: *"Do or do not! There is no 'try!'"*

W.G. Williams
12/30/2005

The Seed...

A successful businessman was growing old and knew it was time to choose a successor to take over the business.

Instead of choosing one of his directors or his children, he decided to do something different. He called all the young executives in his company together. He said, "It's time for me to step down and choose the next CEO. I have decided to choose one of you."

The young executives were shocked, but the boss continued. "I'm going to give each one of you a SEED today - one very special SEED. I want you to plant the seed, water it, and come back here one year from today with what you have grown from the seed I've given you. I'll then judge the plants that you bring and the one I choose will be the next CEO."

One man, Jim, was there that day and he, like the others, received a seed. He went home and excitedly, told his wife the story. She helped him get a pot, soil and compost and he planted the seed. Every day, he would water it and watch to see if it had grown. After about three weeks, some of the other executives began to talk about their seeds and the plants that were beginning to grow.

Jim kept checking his seed, but nothing ever grew. Three weeks, four weeks, five weeks went by, still nothing. By now, others were talking about their plants, but Jim didn't have a plant and he felt like a failure.

Six months went by -- still nothing in Jim's pot. He just knew he had killed his seed. Everyone else had trees and tall plants, but he had nothing. Jim didn't say anything to his colleagues, however. He just kept watering and fertilizing the soil - he so wanted the seed to grow.

A year finally went by, and all the young executives of the company brought their plants to the CEO for inspection. Jim told his wife that he wasn't going to take an empty pot. But she asked him to be honest about what happened.

Jim felt sick to his stomach; it was going to be the most embarrassing moment of his life, but he knew his wife was right. He took his empty pot to the board room. When Jim arrived, he was amazed at the variety of plants grown by the other executives. They were beautiful -- in all shapes and sizes. Jim put his empty pot on the floor and many of his colleagues laughed, a few felt sorry for him!

When the CEO arrived, he surveyed the room and greeted his young executives. Jim just tried to hide in the back...

"My, what great plants, trees, and flowers you have grown," said the CEO. "Today one of you will be appointed the next CEO!"

All of a sudden, the CEO spotted Jim at the back of the room with his empty pot. He ordered the Financial Director to bring him to the front. Jim was terrified. He thought, "The CEO knows I'm a failure! Maybe he'll have me fired!"

When Jim got to the front, the CEO asked him what had happened to his seed - Jim told him the story.

The CEO asked everyone to sit down except Jim. He looked at Jim, and then announced to the young executives, "Behold your next Chief Executive Officer! His name is Jim!"

Jim couldn't believe it. Jim couldn't even grow his seed.

"How could he be the new CEO?" the others said.

Then the CEO said, "One year ago today, I gave everyone in this room a seed. I told you to take the seed, plant it, water it, and bring it back to me today. But I gave you all boiled seeds; they were dead - it was not possible for them to grow.

"All of you, except Jim, have brought me trees and plants and flowers. When you found that the seed would not grow, you substituted another seed for the one I gave you. Jim was the only one with the courage and honesty to bring me a pot with my seed in it. Therefore, he is the one who will be the new Chief Executive Officer!"

* If you plant honesty, you will reap trust
* If you plant goodness, you will reap friends
* If you plant humility, you will reap greatness
* If you plant perseverance, you will reap contentment
* If you plant consideration, you will reap perspective
* If you plant hard work, you will reap success
* If you plant forgiveness, you will reap reconciliation
* If you plant faith in God, you will reap a harvest

So, be careful what you plant now; it will determine what you will reap later. "Whatever You Give to Life, Life Gives You Back!"

Contributed by Gary Thornton
12/22/2009

The Shredder...

A young engineer was leaving the office at 6.45 p.m. when he found the Acting CEO standing in front of a shredder with a piece of paper in his hand.

"Listen," said the Acting CEO, "this is a very sensitive and important document and my secretary is not here. Can you make this thing work?"

"Certainly," said the young engineer. He turned the machine on, inserted the paper, and pressed the start button.

"Excellent, excellent!" said the Acting CEO as his paper disappeared inside the machine, "I just need one copy."

<u>Lesson:</u>
Never, ever assume that your boss knows what he's doing!

Contributed by E.W. Hallford
1/21/2011

The Streaker...

Three ladies are playing the 4th hole at a members-only golf club, when a naked man, wearing a bag over his head, jumped from the trees and ran across the green.

The three ladies looked and were in shock at the size of his manhood.

The first lady commented, "Well, he definitely isn't my husband."

The second lady looked at his manhood and said, "He for sure is not my husband."

The third lady took a good look and said, "He's not even a member of this club!"

Contributed by Harvey West
8/2/2022

The World Is Mine

- Author Unknown -

Today, upon a bus, I saw a very beautiful woman and wished I were as beautiful. When suddenly she rose to leave, I saw her hobble down the aisle. She had one leg and used a crutch. But as she passed, she passed a smile.

Oh, God, forgive me when I whine. I have two legs; the world is mine.

I stopped to buy some candy. The lad who sold it had such charm. I talked with him, he seemed so glad. If I were late, it'd do no harm. And as I left, he said to me, "I thank you, you've been so kind. It's nice to talk with folks like you. You see," he said, "I'm blind."

Oh, God, forgive me when I whine. I have two eyes; the world is mine.

Later while walking down the street, I saw a child I knew. He stood and watched the others play, but he did not know what to do. I stopped a moment and then I said, "Why don't you join them dear?" He looked ahead without a word. I forgot, he couldn't hear.

Oh, God, forgive me when I whine. I have two ears; the world is mine.

With feet to take me where I'd go.
With eyes to see the sunset's glow.
With ears to hear what I'd know.
Oh, God, forgive me when I whine,
I've been blessed indeed, the world is mine.

If this poem makes you feel thankful, forward it to a friend.
After all, it's just a simple reminder that we
have so much to be thankful for.
Give the gift of love. It never comes back empty.
I have been truly blessed with AWESOME FRIENDS
and FAMILY. THE WORLD IS MINE.

Contributed by Susan Luna
10/5/2023

There Comes a Point in Your Life When You Realize...

Who matters…
Who never did…
Who won't anymore…
And who always will.

So, don't worry about people from your past,
There's a reason why they didn't make it to your future.

"To get something you never had, you have
to do something you never did."

When God takes something from your grasp, He's not punishing
you, but merely opening your hands to receive something better.

"The will of God will never take you where the
Grace of God will not protect you."

Contributed by Judy Flahiff
2/8/2011

These People Went Through
Our Educational System...

I handed the teller at my bank a withdrawal slip for $400.00 and said "May I have large bills, please."

She looked at me and said, "I'm sorry sir, all the bills are the same size."

When I got up off the floor, I explained it to her....

When my husband and I arrived at an automobile dealership to pick up our car, we were told the keys had been locked in it. We went to the service department and found a mechanic working feverishly to unlock the driver's side door. As I watched from the passenger side, I instinctively tried the door handle and discovered that it was unlocked.

"Hey!" I announced to the technician, "It's open!"

His reply: "I know. I already got that side."

We had to have the garage door repaired. The repairman told us that one of our problems was that we did not have a 'large' enough motor on the opener.

I thought for a minute and said that we had the largest one available at that time, a 1/2 horsepower.

He shook his head and said, "Lady, you need a 1/4 horsepower."

I responded that 1/2 was larger than 1/4.

He said, "NO, it's not! Four is larger than two."

My daughter and I went through the McDonald's take-out window, and I gave the clerk a $5 bill. Our total was $4.25, so I also handed her a quarter.

She said, "You gave me too much money."

I said, "Yes, I know, but this way you can just give me a dollar bill back."

She sighed and went to get the manager, who asked me to repeat my request.

I did so, and he handed me back the quarter and said, "We're sorry but we could not do that kind of thing."

The clerk then proceeded to give me back $1 and 75 cents in change.

Do not confuse the clerks at McD's.

I live in a semi-rural area. We recently had a new neighbor call the local township administrative office to request the removal of the DEER CROSSING sign on our road.

The reason she gave was, "Too many deer are being hit by cars out here! I don't think this is a good place for them to be crossing anymore."

My daughter went to a local Taco Bell and ordered a taco with "minimal lettuce."

The server said he was sorry, but they only had iceberg lettuce.

I was at the airport, checking in at the gate when an airport employee asked, "Has anyone put anything in your baggage without your knowledge?"

To which I replied, "If it was without my knowledge, how would I know?"

He smiled knowingly and nodded, "That's why we ask."

The stoplight on the corner buzzes when it's safe to cross the street. I was crossing with an intellectually challenged coworker of mine who asked if I knew what the buzzer was for.

I explained that it was a signal to let blind people when the light is red.

Appalled, she responded, "What on earth are blind people doing driving?"

We were at a good-bye luncheon for an old and dear coworker who was leaving the company due to "downsizing," Our manager commented cheerfully, "This is fun. We should do this more often."

Not another word was spoken. We all just looked at each other with that deer-in-the-headlights stare.

I work with an individual who plugged her power strip
back into itself and for the sake of her life, couldn't
understand why her system would not turn on.

How would you pronounce this child's name? "Le-a"
Leah?? NO
Lee - A?? NOPE
Lay - a?? NO
Lei?? Guess Again.

Her mother was irate because everyone was getting her name wrong. It's pronounced "Ledasha."

When the mother was asked about the pronunciation of the name, she said, "De dash don't be silent.

Contributed by Jeanne Zurat
1/25/2011

Things You'll Learn if You Live Long Enough!

It only takes one slow-walking person in the grocery
store to destroy the illusion that I'm a nice person.

***

It turns out that when asked who your favorite child is, you're
supposed to pick out one of your own. I know that now.

***

It's fine to eat a test grape in the produce section, but you take one
bite of rotisserie chicken and it's all, "Sir, you need to leave!"

***

I relabeled all the jars in my wife's spice rack. I'm
not in trouble yet, but the thyme is cumin.

***

I just read a book about marriage that says treat your wife
like you treated her on your first date. So tonight, after
dinner I'm dropping her off at her parent's house.

***

The best way to get back on your feet is to miss two car payments.

***

Driver: "What am I supposed to do with this speeding ticket?"
Officer, "Keep it. When you collect four of them, you get a bicycle."

***

I asked a supermarket employee where they kept the canned peaches.
He said, "I'll see," and then he walked away.
I asked another and she also said, "I'll see," and then walked away.
In the end, I gave up & found them myself, in Aisle C.

***

I told my physical therapist that I broke my arm in two places.
He told me to stop going to those places.

***

When I was a kid, I used to watch the "Wizard of Oz" and
wondered how someone could talk if they didn't have a brain.
Then I got on Facebook.

***

Apparently RSVP'ing to a wedding invitation with
"Maybe next time" isn't the correct response?

***

I just burned 1,200 calories. I forgot the pizza in the oven.

Contributed by Dennis Bialecki
10/26/2023

This is A Keeper

I grew up with practical parents. A mother, God love her, who washed aluminum foil after she cooked in it, then reused it. She was the original recycle queen before they had a name for it. A father who was happier getting old shoes fixed than buying new ones.

Their marriage was good, their dreams focused. Their best friends lived barely a wave away.

I can see them now, Dad in trousers, tee shirt and a hat and Mom in a house dress, lawn mower in one hand, and dishtowel in the other. It was the time for fixing things. A curtain rod, the kitchen radio, screen door, the oven door, the hem in a dress. Things we keep.

It was a way of life, and sometimes it made me crazy. All that re-fixing, eating, renewing, I wanted just once to be wasteful. Waste meant affluence. Throwing things away meant you knew there'd always be more.

But then my mother died, and on that clear summer's night, in the warmth of the hospital room, I was struck with the pain of learning that sometimes there isn't any more.

Sometimes, what we care about most gets all used up and goes away ... never to return. So ... While we have it ... it's best we love it ... And care for it ... And fix it when it's broken ... And heal it when it's sick.

This is true. For marriage ... And old cars ... And children with bad report cards ... And dogs with bad hips ... And aging parents ... And grandparents. We keep them because they are worth it, because we are worth it.

Some things we keep. Like a best friend that moved away or a classmate we grew up with.

There are just some things that make life important, like people we know who are special ... And so, we keep them close!

I received this from someone who thinks I am a "keeper," so I've sent it to the people I think of in the same way ... Now it's your turn to send to those people who are "keepers in YOUR life.

Good friends are like stars … you don't always see them, but they are always there. Keep them close!

Contributed by Susan Luna
6/5/2023

To Understand a Military Veteran, You Must Know ...

We left home as teenagers or in our early
twenties for an unknown adventure.
We loved our country enough to defend it
and protect it with our own lives.
We said goodbye to friends and family and everything we knew.
We learned the basics and then we scattered in
the wind to the far corners of the Earth.
We found new friends and new family.
We became brothers and sisters regardless of color, race or creed.
We had plenty of good times, and plenty of bad times.
We didn't get enough sleep.
We smoked and drank too much.
We picked up both good and bad habits.
We worked hard and played harder.
We didn't earn a great wage.
We experienced the happiness of mail call and the
sadness of missing important events.
We didn't know when, or even if, we were ever going to see home again.
We grew up fast, and yet somehow, we never grew up at all.
We fought for our freedom, as well as the freedom of others.
Some of us saw actual combat, and some of us didn't.
Some of us saw the world, and some of us didn't.
Some of us dealt with physical warfare, most of
us dealt with psychological warfare.
We have seen and experienced and dealt with things that we can't
fully describe or explain, as not all of our sacrifices were physical.
We participated in time honored ceremonies and rituals with
each other, strengthening our bonds and camaraderie.

We counted on each other to get our job done
and sometimes to survive it at all.
We have dealt with victory and tragedy.
We have celebrated and mourned.
We lost a few along the way.
When our adventure was over, some of us went back home, some of
us started somewhere new and some of us never came home at all.
We have told amazing and hilarious stories of our exploits and adventures.
We share an unspoken bond with each other, that most
people don't experience, and few will understand.
We speak highly of our own branch of service,
and poke fun at the other branches.
We know, however, that, if needed, we will be there for our
brothers and sisters and stand together as one, in a heartbeat.
Being a Veteran is something that had to be
earned, and it can never be taken away.
It has no monetary value, but at the same time it is a priceless gift.
People see a Veteran and they thank them for their service.
When we see each other, we give that little upwards head
nod, or a slight smile, knowing that we have shared and
experienced things that most people have not.
So, from myself to the rest of the veterans out there, I commend and
thank you for all that you have done and sacrificed for your country.
Try to remember the good times and make peace with the bad times.
Share your stories.
(Copied from an unknown author)

Contributed by David A. Silverman
11/11/2021

Today's Geometry Class

Contributed by James Teiper
5/4/2024

Traffic Fines...

One Swedish motorist could be facing a gargantuan speeding fine — up to $962,000 — after he was caught driving 180 mph along a Swiss motorway.

Police seized the Swede's driver's license and 570-horsepower black Mercedes-Benz after he was released from police custody. He could face a penalty of up to 1 million Swiss francs — or $962,000. In Switzerland speeding fines are based on the severity of the offense and the offender's income level.

Police said the 37-year-old motorist was driving so fast in his $240,000 sports car that it took him nearly half a mile to stop.

Swiss officials did not know if it was a record, but that it "looks very close to one," federal roads office spokesman Thomas Rohrbach said. "We have no record of anyone being caught traveling faster in the country," a police spokesman told Britain's Daily Telegraph.

The driver's explanation to officers: "I think the speedo on the car, which is new, is faulty."

A speed camera on the A12 highway between Bern and Lausanne captured the transgression. Police said he had eluded being zapped by numerous radars en route simply because he was going too fast and they were unable to clock speeds beyond 125 mph. A newer camera perched along the motorway was able to snap his offense.

It's not the first time someone has had to pay such a hefty fine in Europe for speeding. And even lower speeds can generate big fines.

A Swiss court slapped a $290,000 speeding ticket on a millionaire Ferrari driver who drove 60 mph (nearly twice the 30-mph limit) through a small village.

The head of Finnish communications giant Nokia was ordered to pay a $103,000 fine for his speeding ticket in 2002. Officers pulled over Anssi Vanjoki on his cherry red Harley Davidson in Helsinki after he was clocked driving 47 mph in a 31-mph zone.

In Finland, traffic fines are also proportionate to an offender's crime and income level. In addition, being caught driving after even one beer or glass of wine results in the driver's car being confiscated. In Finland you see a lot of people leaving bars on foot.

Contributed by David A. Silverman
8/12/2010

<u>Tragic news from up North . . ..</u>
MERRY CHRISTMAS . . .

Contributed by Jaton West
12/28/2010

Tragic Domain Names

Who Represents?
A database for agencies to the rich and famous:
(*http://www.whorepresents.com*)

Experts Exchange
A knowledge base where programmers can exchange advice and views:
(*http://www.expertsexchange.com*)

Looking for a pen?
- Look no further than Pen Island:
(*http://www.penisland.net*)

Need a therapist?
(*http://www.therapistfinder.com*)

Mole Station
– A Native Nursery, based in New South Wales, Australia:
(*http://www.molestationnursery.com*)

New to Milan, Italy and you need electric light?
Why not sign up on-line with Power-Gen?
(http://www.powergenitalia.com)

Contributed by James Teiper
3/6/2006

Two Brothers...

Two brothers, 8 and 10, were excessively mischievous. They were always getting into trouble and their parents knew that if any mischief occurred in their town, their two boys were probably involved.

The boys' mother heard that a preacher in town had been successful in disciplining children, so she asked if he would speak with her boys. The preacher agreed, but he asked to see them individually.

The mother sent the 8-year-old in the morning, with the older boy to see the preacher in the afternoon. The preacher, a huge man with a deep booming voice, sat the younger boy down and asked him sternly, "Do you know where God is, son?"

The boy's mouth dropped open, but he made no response, sitting there wide-eyed with his mouth hanging open.

So, the preacher repeated the question in an even sterner tone, "Where is God!"

Again, the boy made no attempt to answer. The preacher raised his voice even more and shook his finger in the boy's face and bellowed, "WHERE IS GOD?"

The boy screamed and bolted from the room, ran directly home and dove into his closet, slamming the door behind him.

When his older brother found him in the closet, he asked, "What happened?"

The younger brother, gasping for breath, replied, "We are in BIG trouble this time!" "GOD is missing, and they think WE did it!"

Contributed by Judy Flahiff
9/23/2010

Veterans' Day Tribute...

The elderly parking lot attendant wasn't in a good mood.

Neither was Sam Bierstock. It was around 1 a.m., and Bierstock, a Delray Beach, Florida, eye doctor, business consultant, corporate speaker, and musician, was bone tired after appearing at an event. He pulled up in his car, and the parking attendant began to speak. "I took two bullets for this country and look what I'm doing," he said bitterly.

At first, Bierstock didn't know what to say to the World War II veteran. But he rolled down his window and told the man, "Really, from the bottom of my heart, I want to thank you." Then the old soldier began to cry. "That really got to me," Bierstock says.

Cut to today.

Bierstock, 58, and John Melnick, 54, of Pompano Beach - a member of Bierstock's band, Dr. Sam and the Managed Care Band - have written a song inspired by that old soldier in the airport parking lot. The mournful "Before You Go" does more than salute those who fought in WWII. It encourages people to go out of their way to thank the aging warriors before they die.

"If we had lost that particular war, our whole way of life would have been shot," says Bierstock, who plays harmonica. "Every ethnic minority would be dead. And the soldiers are now dying at the rate of about 2,000 every day. I thought we needed to thank them."

The song is striking a chord and within days Bierstock had placed it on the Web (www.beforeyougo.us). "It made me cry," wrote one veteran's son. Another sent an e-mail saying that only after his father consumed several glasses of wine would he discuss "the unspeakable horrors" he and other soldiers had witnessed in places such as Anzio, Iwo Jima, Bataan, and Omaha Beach. "I can never thank them enough," the son wrote. "Thank you for thinking about them."

Bierstock and Melnick thought about shipping it off to a professional singer, maybe a Lee Greenwood type, but because time was running out for so many veterans, they decided it was best to release it quickly, for free, on the Web. They've sent the song to Sen. John McCain and others in Washington. Already they have been invited to perform it in Houston for a Veterans Day tribute - this after just a few days on the Web. They hope every veteran in America gets a chance to hear it.

Contributed by Susan Luna
11/14/2005

Want To Buy a Watch?

If you were in the market for a watch in 1880, would you know where to get one? You would go to a store, right? Well, of course you could do that, but if you wanted one that was cheaper and a bit better than most of the store watches, you went to the train station! Sound a bit funny? Well, for about 500 towns across the northern United States, that's where the best watches were found.

Why were the best watches found at the train station? The railroad company wasn't selling the watches, not at all. The telegraph operator was. Most of the time the telegraph operator was located in the railroad station because the telegraph lines followed the railroad tracks from town to town. It was usually the shortest distance and the rights-of-way had already been secured for the rail line.

Most of the station agents were also skilled telegraph operators and that was the primary way that they communicated with the railroad. They would know when trains left the previous station and when they were due at their next station. And it was the telegraph operator who had the watches. As a matter of fact they sold more of them than almost all the stores combined for a period of about nine years.

This was all arranged by "Richard," who was a telegraph operator himself. He was on duty in the North Redwood, Minnesota train station one day when a load of watches arrived from the East. It was a huge crate of pocket watches. No one ever came to claim them.

So, Richard sent a telegram to the manufacturer and asked them what they wanted to do with the watches. The manufacturer didn't want to pay the freight back, so they wired Richard to see if he could sell them. So, Richard did. He sent a wire to every agent in the system asking them if they wanted a cheap, but good, pocket watch. He sold the entire case in less than two days and at a handsome profit.

That started it all. He ordered more watches from the watch company and encouraged the telegraph operators to set up a display case in the station offering high quality watches for a cheap price to all the travelers. It worked! It didn't take long for the word to spread and, before long, people other than travelers came to the train station to buy watches.

Richard became so busy that he had to hire a professional watch maker to help him with the orders. That was Alvah. And the rest is history as they say. The business took off and soon expanded to many other lines of dry goods.

Richard and Alvah left the train station and moved their company to Chicago -- and it's still there.

It's a little-known fact that for a while in the 1880's, the biggest watch retailer in the country was at the train station. It all started with a telegraph operator: Richard Sears and his partner Alvah Roebuck!

from David Taylor
10/11/2022

Washing Clothes...

Years ago, an Alabama grandmother gave the new bride directions for washing clothes. A copy was found in an old scrapbook - - and here it is with spelling errors and all.

* * * * * * * * *

*   Build fire in backyard to heat kettle of rain water.
*   Set tubs so smoke wont blow in eyes if wind is pert.
*   Shave one hole cake of lie soap in boilin' water.
*   Sort things, make 3 piles
       1 pile white,
       1 pile colored,
       1 pile work britches and rags.

* To make starch, stir flour in cool water to smooth,
       then thin down with boiling water.

* Take white things, rub dirty spots on board, scrub hard, and boil,
then rub colored don't boil the colored -- just wrench and starch.

* Take things out of kettle with broom stick
       handle, then wrench, and starch.

* Hang old rags on fence.

* Spread tea towels on grass.

* Pore wrench water in flower bed. Scrub porch with
       hot soapy water. Turn tubs upside down.

* Go put on clean dress, smooth hair with hair combs. Brew cup of tea, sit and rock a spell and count your blessings.

==

Paste this over your washer and dryer. The next time you think things are bleak, read it again, kiss that washing machine and dryer, and give thanks. First thing each morning you should run and hug your washer and dryer, also your toilet---those two-holers used to get mighty cold!

For you non-southerners, "wrench" means rinse.

...And those were the "Good Old Days!"

Contributed by Bubba & Bonnie Mehling
10/3/2006

Welcome To Texas...

Dear Diary:
I just moved to Texas! Now this is a state that knows how to live!! Beautiful sunny days and warm balmy evenings.
What a place! It is beautiful. I've finally found my home. I love it here.

June 14th:
Really heating up. Got to 100 today. Not a problem. Live in an air-conditioned home, drive an air-conditioned car. What a pleasure to see the sun everyday like this. I'm turning into a sun worshipper.

June 30th:
Had the backyard landscaped with western plants today. Lots of cactus and rocks. What a breeze to maintain. No more mowing the lawn for me. Another scorcher today, but I love it here.

July 10th:
The temperature hasn't been below 100 all week. How do people get used to this kind of heat? At least, it's kind of windy though. But getting used to the heat is taking longer than I expected.

July 15th:
Fell asleep by the community pool. (Got 3rd degree burns over 60% of my body). Missed 3 days of work. What a dumb thing to do. I learned my lesson though. Got to respect the ol' sun in a climate like this.

July 20th:
I missed Lomita (my cat) sneaking into the car when I left this morning. By the time I got to the hot car at noon, Lomita had died and swollen up to the size of a shopping bag, then popped like a water balloon. The car now smells like Kibbles and $hits.

I learned my lesson though. No more pets in this heat. Good ol' Mr Sun strikes again.

July 25th:
The wind sucks. It feels like a giant freaking blow dryer!! And it's hot as hell.
The home air-conditioner is on the Fritz and the AC repairman charged $200 just to drive by and tell me he needed to order parts.

July 30th:
Been sleeping outside on the patio for 3 nights now. $225,000 house and I can't even go inside. Lomita is the lucky one.
Why did I ever come here?

Aug. 4th:
It's 115 degrees. Finally got the air-conditioner fixed today. It cost $500 and gets the temperature down to 85.
I hate this stupid state.

Aug. 8th:
If another wise a$$ cracks, 'Hot enough for you today?' I'm going to strangle him...
D@mn heat!
By the time I get to work, the radiator is boiling over, my clothes are soaking wet, and I smell like baked cat!!

Aug. 9th:
Tried to run some errands after work. Wore shorts, and when I sat on the seats in the car, I thought my a$$ was on fire. My skin melted to the seat. I lost 2 layers of flesh and all the hair on the back of my legs and a$$ . . .
Now my car smells like burnt hair, fried a$$, and baked cat.

Aug. 20th:
The weather report might as well be a d@mn recording. Hot and sunny... Hot and sunny...Hot and sunny...It's been too hot to do $hit for 2 d@mn months and the weatherman says it might really warm up next week.
Doesn't it ever rain in this d@mn state?

Water rationing will be next, so my $1700 worth of cactus will just dry up and blow over. Even the cactus can't live in this d@mn heat.

Aug. 24th:
Welcome to HELL! Temperature got to 115 today. Cactus are dead. Forgot to crack the window and blew the d@mn windshield out of the car. The installer came to fix it and guess what he asked me???
"Hot enough for you today?"
My sister had to spend $1,500 to bail me out of jail.
Freaking Texas…What kind of a sick demented idiot would want to live here??
Will write later to let you know how the trial goes…

Contributed by Eddie Kay Nichols
9/1/2006

What A Difference A Century Makes!

Here are some of the U.S. statistics for the Year 1906:

* The average life expectancy in the U.S. was 47.
* Only 14 percent of the homes in the U.S. had a bathtub.
* Only 8 percent of the homes had a telephone.
* A three-minute call from Denver to New York City cost eleven dollars.
* There were only 8,000 cars in the U.S., and only 144 miles of paved roads.
* The maximum speed limit in most cities was 10 mph.
* Alabama, Mississippi, Iowa, and Tennessee each were more heavily populated than California. With a mere 1.4 million people, California was only the 21st most populous state in the Union.
* The tallest structure in the world was the Eiffel Tower.
* The average wage in the U.S. was 22 cents per hour.
* The average U.S. worker made between $200 and $500 per year.
* A competent accountant could expect to earn $2,000 per year, a dentist $2,500 per year, a veterinarian between $1,500 and $4,000 per year, and a mechanical engineer about $5,000 per year.
* More than 95 percent of all births in the U.S. took place at <u>home.</u>
* Ninety percent of all U.S. doctors had no college education. Instead, they attended so-called medical schools, many of which were condemned in the press and by the government as "substandard."
* Sugar cost four cents a pound.
* Eggs were fourteen cents a dozen.
* Coffee was fifteen cents a pound.
* Most women only washed their hair once a month and used borax or egg yolks for shampoo.

* Canada passed a law that prohibited poor people from entering into their country for any reason.
* The five leading causes of death in the U.S. were:
    1. Pneumonia and influenza
    2. Tuberculosis
    3. Diarrhea
    4. Heart disease
    5. Stroke

* The American flag had 45 stars. Arizona, Oklahoma, New Mexico, Hawaii, and Alaska hadn't been admitted to the Union yet.
* The population of Las Vegas, Nevada, was only 30.
* Crossword puzzles, canned beer, and ice tea hadn't been invented yet.
* There was no Mother's Day or Father's Day.
* Two out of every 10 U.S. adults couldn't read or write.
* Only 6 percent of all Americans had graduated from high school.
* Marijuana, heroin, and morphine were all available over the counter at the local corner drugstores. Back then pharmacist said, "Heroin clears the complexion, gives buoyancy to the mind, regulates the stomach and bowels, and is, in fact, a perfect guardian of health."
* Eighteen percent of households in the U.S. had at least one full-time servant or domestic help.
* There were about 230 reported murders in the entire U.S.

Contributed by David Taylor
2/8/2006

What A Typo Can Do...

A young monk arrived at the monastery and was assigned to helping the other monks in copying the old canons and laws of the church by hand.

He noticed, however, that all of the monks were copying from copies, not from the original manuscript. So, the new monk went to the head abbot to question this.

He pointed out that if someone made even a small error in the first copy, it would never be picked up! In fact, that error would be continued in all of the subsequent copies.

The head monk, said, "We've been copying from the copies for centuries, but you make a good point, my son."

He went down into the dark caves underneath the monastery
where the original manuscripts were held as archives in a locked
vault that hadn't been opened for hundreds of years.
Hours went by and nobody saw the old abbot.

So, the young monk got worried and went down to look for him.
He found him banging his head against the wall and wailing,
"We missed the R!
We missed the R!
We missed the R!"
His forehead was all bloody and bruised and he was crying uncontrollably.
The young monk asked the old abbot, "What's wrong, father?"
With A choking voice, the old abbot replied,
«The word was...

CELEBRATE!

Contributed by Ron Heisler
2/23/2011

What is a Veteran?

Father Dennis Edward O'Brien, USMC

Some veterans bear visible signs of their service: a missing limb, a jagged scar, a certain look in the eye. Others may carry the evidence inside them: a pin holding a bone together, a piece of shrapnel in the leg - or perhaps another sort of inner steel: the soul's ally forged in the refinery of adversity. Except in parades, however, the men and women who have kept America safe wear no badge or emblem. You can't tell a vet just by looking.

He is the cop on the beat who spent six months in Saudi Arabia sweating two gallons a day making sure the armored personnel carriers didn't run out of fuel.

He is the bar room loudmouth, dumber than five wooden planks, whose overgrown frat-boy behavior is outweighed a hundred times in the cosmic scales by four hours of exquisite bravery near the 38th parallel.

She or he—is the nurse who fought against futility and went to sleep sobbing every night for two solid years in Da Nang.

He is the POW who went away one person and came back another— or didn't come back AT ALL.

He is the Quantico drill instructor who has never seen combat—but has saved countless lives by turning slouchy, no-account rednecks and gang members into Marines, and teaching them to watch each other's backs.

He is the parade-riding Legionnaire who pins on his ribbons and medals with a prosthetic hand.

He is the career quartermaster who watches the ribbons and medals pass him by.

He is one of the three anonymous heroes in The Tomb of The Unknowns, whose presence at the Arlington National Cemetery must forever preserve the memory of all the anonymous heroes whose valor dies unrecognized with them on the battlefield or in the ocean's sunless deep.

He is the old guy bagging groceries at the supermarket—palsied now and aggravatingly slow—who helped liberate a Nazi death camp and who wishes all day long that his wife were still alive to hold him when the nightmares come.

He is an ordinary and yet an extraordinary human being—a person who offered some of his life's most vital years in the service of his country, and who sacrificed his ambitions so others would not have to sacrifice theirs.

He is a soldier and a savior and a sword against the darkness, and he is nothing more than the finest, greatest testimony on behalf of the finest, greatest nation ever known.

So remember, each time you see someone who has served our country, just lean over and say Thank You. That's all most people need, and in most cases, it will mean more than any medals they could have been awarded or were awarded.

Two little words that mean a lot, "THANK YOU."

Contributed by Bubba & Bonnie Mehling
11/20/2006

What's A Penny Worth?

You always hear the usual stories of pennies on the sidewalk being good luck, gifts from angels, etc. This is the first time I've ever heard this twist on the story. It gives you something to think about.

Several years ago, a friend of mine and her husband were invited to spend the weekend at the home of her husband's employer. My friend, Arlene, was nervous about the weekend. The boss was very wealthy with a fine home on the waterway and cars costing more than her house.

The first day and evening went well, and Arlene was delighted to have this rare glimpse into how the very wealthy live. Her husband's employer was quite generous as a host and took them to the finest restaurants. Arlene knew she would never have the opportunity to indulge in this kind of extravagance again, so was enjoying herself immensely.

As the three of them were about to enter an exclusive restaurant one evening, the boss was walking slightly ahead of Arlene and her husband. He stopped suddenly, looking down on the pavement for a long, silent moment. Arlene wondered if she was supposed to pass him. There was nothing on the ground except a single darkened penny that someone had dropped and a few cigarette butts. Still silent, the man reached down and picked up the penny. He held it up and smiled, then put it in his pocket as if he had found a great treasure.

How absurd! What need did this man have for a single penny? Why would he even take the time to stop and pick it up?

Throughout dinner, the entire scene nagged at her. Finally, she could stand it no longer. She casually mentioned that her daughter once had a coin collection and asked if the penny he had found had been of some value.

A smile crept across the man's face as he reached into his pocket for the penny and held it out for her to see. She had seen many pennies before! What was the point of this?

"Look at it," he said. "Read what it says."

She read the words, «United States of America...»

"No, not that. Read further."

"One cent?"

«No, keep reading.»

"In God we Trust?"

«Yes!»

«And?»

"And if I trust in God, the name of God is holy, even on a coin. Whenever I find a coin, I see that inscription. It is written on every single United States coin, but we never seem to notice it! God drops a message right in front of me telling me to trust Him. Who am I to pass it by? When I see a coin, I pray. I stop to see if my trust IS in God at that moment. I pick the coin up as a response to God; that I do trust in Him. For a short time, at least, I cherish it as if it were gold. I think it is God's way of starting a conversation with me. Lucky for me, God is patient and pennies are plentiful!"

When I was out shopping today, I found a penny on the sidewalk. I stopped and picked it up and realized that I had been worrying and fretting in my mind about things I cannot change. I read the words, "In God We Trust," and had to laugh. "Yes, God, I get the message!"

It seems that I've been finding an inordinate number of pennies in the last few months, but then, pennies are plentiful! And God is patient.

Contributed by Sherry Neise
10/14/2009

What's Your Handicap?

A businessman was attending a conference in Africa. He had a free day and wanted to play a round of golf and was directed to a golf course in the nearby jungle. After a short journey, he arrived at the course and asked the pro if he could get on.

"Sure," said the pro, "What's your handicap?"

Not wanting to admit that he had an 18 handicap, he decided to cut it a bit. "Well, it's 16," said the businessman, "but what's the relevance since I'll be playing alone?"

"It's very important for us to know," said the pro, who then called a caddy. "Go out with this gentleman," said the pro, "his handicap is 16."

The businessman was very surprised at this constant reference to his handicap. The caddy picked up the businessman's bag and a large rifle. Again, the businessman was surprised but decided to ask no questions. They arrived on the 1st hole, a par-4.

"It's wise to avoid those trees on the left," said the caddy.

Needless to say, the businessman duck-hooked his ball into the trees. He found his ball and was about to punch it out when he heard the loud crack of the rifle and a large snake fell dead from a tree above his head.

The caddy stood next to him with the rifle smoking in his hand. "That's the Black Mamba, the most poisonous snake in all Africa. You're lucky I was here with you."

After taking a bogey, they moved to the 2nd hole, a par-5. "Good to avoid those bushes on the right," says the caddy.

Of course, the businessman's ball went straight into the bushes. As he went to pick up his ball, he heard the loud crack of the caddy's rifle once again, and a huge lion fell dead at his feet.

"I've saved your life again," said the caddy.

The 3rd hole was a par-3 with a lake in front of the green. The businessman's ball came up just short of the green and rolled back to the edge of the water. To take a shot, he had to stand with one foot in the lake. As he was about to swing, a large crocodile emerged from the water and bit off much of his right leg.

As he fell to the ground bleeding and in great pain, he saw the caddy with the rifle propped at his side, looking on unconcernedly as they waited for the medics.

"Why didn't you shoot it?" asked the man incredulously.

"I'm sorry, sir," said the caddy. "This is the 17th handicap hole. You don't get a shot here."

And that, my golfing friends, is why you should never lie about your handicap!

From Ron Gargasz
7/27/2012

Who's On First?

After having dug to a depth of 10 meters last year, Italian scientists found traces of copper wire dating back 200 years and came to the conclusion that their ancestors already had a telephone network more than 200 years ago.

Not to be outdone by the Italians, in the weeks that followed, Irish scientists dug to a depth of 20 meters, and shortly after, headlines in the Irish newspapers read: "Irish archaeologists have found traces of 300 year old copper wire and have concluded that their ancestors already had an advanced high-tech communications network a hundred years earlier than the Italians."

One week later, "The Daily Zgoda," a Warsaw newspaper, reported that after digging as deep as 30 meters in corn fields near Krakow, Stanley Skrzepcynski, a self taught archeologist, reported that he found absolutely nothing."

"Skrzepcynski has therefore concluded that 400 years ago Poles were already using wireless."

Contributed by Bubba & Bonnie Mehling
10/25/2007

Who's Your Daddy?

***The following are all replies that women have written
on Child Support Agency forms in the section for listing
"father's details;" or putting it another way,
"Who's your Daddy?" These are genuine excerpts from those forms.***

1. Regarding the identity of the father of my twins -- child A was fathered by Jim Munson. I am unsure as to the identity of the father of child B, but I believe that he was conceived on the same night.

2. I am unsure, as to the identity of the father of my child as I was being sick out of a window when taken unexpectedly from behind. I can provide you with a list of names of men that I think were at the party if this helps.

3. I do not know the name of the father of my little girl. She was conceived at a party at 3600 East Grand Boulevard where I had unprotected sex with a man I met that night. I do remember that the sex was so good that I fainted. If you do manage to track down the father, can you send me his phone number? Thanks.

4. I don't know the identity of the father of my daughter. He drives a BMW that now has a hole made by my stiletto in one of the door panels. Perhaps you can contact BMW service stations in this area and see if he's had it replaced.

5. I have never had sex with a man. I am still a Virginian. I am awaiting a letter from the Pope confirming that my son's conception was ejaculate and that he is the Saver risen again.

6. I cannot tell you the name of child A's dad as he informs me that to do so would blow his cover and that would have cataclysmic implications for the economy. I am torn between doing right by you and right by the country. Please advise.

7. I do not know who the father of my child was as all look the same to me.

8. Peter Smith Is the father of child A. If you do catch up with him, can you ask him what he did with my AC/DC CDs? Child B who was also borned at the same time...well, I don't have clue.

9. From the dates it seems that my daughter was conceived at Disney World; maybe it really is the Magic Kingdom.

10. So much about that night is a blur. The only thing that I remember for sure is Delia Smith did a program about eggs earlier in the evening. If I had stayed in and watched more TV rather than going to the party at 8956 Miller Ave, mine might have remained unfertilized.

11. I am unsure as to the identity of the father of my baby, after all, like when you eat a can of beans you can't be sure which one made you fart.

Contributed by Gary Thornton
2/27/2024

Who Was the First President of the United States?

Think back to your history books - The United States
declared its independence in 1776, yet George Washington
did not take office until April 30, 1789.
So, who was running the country during these
initial years of our young country?
In fact, the first President of the United States was named John Hanson!
I can hear you now -John who?
John Hanson was the first President of The United States.

There was also a U.S. stamp made in his honor. The new country was actually formed on March 1, 1781, with the adoption of The Articles of Confederation. This document was actually proposed on June 11, 1776, but not agreed upon by Congress until November 15, 1777.

Maryland refused to sign this document until Virginia and New York ceded their western lands (Maryland was afraid that these states would gain too much power in the new government from such large amounts of land).

Once the signing took place in 1781, a President was needed to run the country. John Hanson was chosen unanimously by Congress (which included George Washington). In fact, all the other potential candidates refused to run against him, as he was a major player in the revolution and an extremely influential member of Congress.

As the first President, Hanson had quite the shoes to fill. No one had ever been President and the role was poorly defined. His actions in office would set precedent for all future Presidents. He took office just as the Revolutionary War ended.

Almost immediately, the troops demanded to be paid. As would be expected after any long war, there were no funds to meet the salaries. As a result, the soldiers threatened to overthrow the new government and put Washington on the throne as a monarch.

All the members of Congress ran for their lives, leaving Hanson as the only guy left running the government. He somehow managed to calm the troops down and hold the country together. If he had failed, the government would have fallen almost immediately, and everyone would have been bowing to King Washington.

Hanson, as President, ordered all foreign troops off American soil, as well as the removal of all foreign flags. This was quite the feat, considering the fact that so many European countries had a stake in the United States since the days following Columbus.

Hanson established the Great Seal of the United States, which all Presidents have since been required to use on all official documents. President Hanson also established the first Treasury Department, the first Secretary of War, and the first Foreign Affairs Department.

Lastly, he declared that the fourth Thursday of every November was to be Thanksgiving Day, which is still true today.

The Articles of Confederation only allowed a President to serve a one-year term during any three year period, so Hanson actually accomplished quite a bit in such little time. Seven other presidents were elected after him:

1. John Hanson

2. Elias Boudinot (1782-83),

3. Thomas Mifflin (1783-84),

4. Richard Henry Lee (1784-85),

5. John Hancock (1785-86),

6. Nathan Gorman (1786-87),

7. Arthur St. Clair (1787-88), and

8. Cyrus Griffin (1788-89).

All served prior to George Washington ever taking office.

So, what happened? Why don't we hear about the first eight presidents?

It's quite simple - The Articles of Confederation didn't work well. The individual states had too much power, and nothing could be agreed upon. A new doctrine needed to be written - something we know as the Constitution.

And that leads us to the end of our story. George Washington definitely was NOT the first President of the United States. He was the first President of the United States under the Constitution we follow today.

And the first eight Presidents have been largely forgotten in history.

Contributed by Judy Flahiff
5/8/2024

Why Men Are Happier...

Men are just happier people -- What do you expect from such simple creatures? Your last name stays put. The garage is all yours. Wedding plans take care of themselves. Chocolate is just another snack.

You can be President. You can never be pregnant. You can wear a white T-shirt to a water park. You can wear NO shirt to a water park. Car mechanics tell you the truth.

The world is your urinal. You never have to drive to another gas station restroom because this one is just too icky. You don't have to stop and think of which way to turn a nut on a bolt. Same work, more pay. Wrinkles add character. Wedding dress $5000. Tux rental-$100. People never stare at your chest when you're talking to them.

The occasional well-rendered belch is practically expected. New shoes don't cut, blister, or mangle your feet. One mood all the time. Phone conversations are over in 30 seconds flat. You know stuff about tanks. A five-day vacation requires only one suitcase. You can open all your own jars. You get extra credit for the slightest act of thoughtfulness. If someone forgets to invite you, he or she can still be your friend.

Your underwear is $8.95 for a three-pack. Three pairs of shoes are more than enough. You almost never have strap problems in public. You are unable to see wrinkles in your clothes. Everything on your face stays its original color. The same hairstyle lasts for years, maybe decades. You only have to shave your face and neck.

You can play with toys all your life. Your belly usually hides your big hips. One wallet and one pair of shoes one color for all seasons. You can wear shorts no matter how your legs look. You can "do" your nails with a pocketknife. You have freedom of choice concerning growing a mustache.

You can do Christmas shopping for 25 relatives on December 24 in 25 minutes.

No wonder men are happier!

Contributed by Gary Thornton
6/22/2006

Why Women Make Better Assassins

The CIA had an opening for an assassin.

After all the background checks, interviews and testing were done, there were three finalists: two men and a woman.

For the final test, the CIA agents took one of the men to a large metal door and handed him a gun. "We must know that you will follow your instructions no matter what the circumstances. Inside the room you will find your wife sitting in a chair. Kill her."

The man said, "You can't be serious. I could never shoot my wife."

The agent said, "Then you are not the right man for this job. Take your wife and go home."

The second man was given the same instructions. He took the gun and went into the room. All was quiet for about five minutes. The man came out with tears in his eyes. "I tried, but I can't kill my wife."

The agent said, "You don't have what it takes, so take your wife and go home."

Finally, it was the woman's turn. She was given the same instructions: to kill her husband. She took the gun and went into the room. Shots were heard one after another. They heard screaming, crashing, and banging on the walls.

After a few minutes, all was quiet.

The door opened slowly and there stood the woman, wiping sweat from her brow. "The gun was loaded with blanks" she said. "I had to beat him to death with the chair."

Contributed by Judy Flahiff
9/27/2023

Winter in Minnesota!

I just got off the phone with a friend in Minnesota. He said that since early this morning the snow has been falling. Now it's waist high and is still coming down.

The temperature has dropped to below zero and the north wind is increasing.

His wife has done nothing but look through the kitchen window all day.

He says that if it gets much worse, he may have to let her in.

Contributed by E.W. Hallford
1/14/2011

Wisdom in Beer

"Sometimes, when I reflect on all the beer I drink, I feel ashamed. Then I look into the glass and think about the workers in the brewery and all of their hopes and dreams. If I didn't drink this beer, they might be out of work and their dreams would be shattered. I think it's better to drink this beer and let dreams come true, than be selfish & worry about my liver."
Babe Ruth

"When I read about the evils of drinking, I gave up reading."
Paul Horning

"24 hours in a day and 24 beers in a case.
Coincidence? I think not!"
H. L. Mencken

"When we drink, we get drunk. When we get drunk, we fall asleep.
When we fall asleep, we commit no sin. When
we commit no sin, we go to heaven.
So, let's all get drunk and go to heaven."
George Bernard Shaw

"Beer is proof that God loves us and wants us to be happy."
Benjamin Franklin

"Without question, the greatest invention in
the history of mankind is beer.
Oh, I grant you that the wheel was also a fine invention,
but the wheel does not go nearly as well with pizza."
Dave Barry

"Beer: Helping ugly people have sex since 3000 B.C."
W. C. Fields

"Remember 'I' before 'E,' except in Budweiser."
Professor Irwin Corey

"To some it is a six-pack. To me, it is a Support
Group ... Salvation in a can."
Leo Durocher

One night at **Cheers,** a TV Sitcom,
Cliff Clavin said to his buddy, Norm Peterson: "Well, ya-see, Normy,
it's like this. A herd of buffalo can only move as fast as the slowest
buffalo. And when the herd is hunted, it's the slowest and weakest
ones at the back that're killed first. This natural selection is good
for the herd as a whole, because the general speed and health of the
whole group keeps improving by the regular killing of the weakest
members. In much the same way, the human brain can only operate
as fast as the slowest brain cells. Excessive intake of alcohol, as we

know, kills brain cells but, naturally, it attacks the slowest and weakest brain cells first. In this way, regular consumption of beer eliminates the weaker brain cells, making the brain a faster and more efficient machine. That's why you always feel smarter after a few beers!"

Contributed by Dennis Bialecki
10/31/2023

The Wonders of Traveling
with E-Mail in 2005

When I planned this trip to the west coast, I thought that keeping up with my e-mails would be a piece of cake. Everywhere I looked, I saw hotels advertising "High Speed Internet Connections" so how hard could it be?

Harder than I would have thought!

How about the hotel that offered High Speed Internet Connections ... but at $2.50 for five minutes!

Or the hotel whose idea of "high speed" is 54k through a dial-up connections? And then their phone system cut off calls after 10 minutes which doesn't help much when you have 15 minutes of downloading. Every time you re-dial, the ISP starts all over again.

And I also discovered a new trick being used to deter people who wander around looking for a wi-fi hotspot (like outside a hotel). Somehow a signal can come back that burns out your wireless card when you have not been given permission to use it -- even though it shows up as "open access." Technogeeks tell me that it can't be done but I had a card burned out in Texas and another one burned out in California.

Tonight, I'm trying to get caught up from a Holiday Inn in Reno. They have wireless access ... but only in the lobby. They do have high speed access in the rooms but with a LAN modem in each room ... and it works well.

The moral is that if you want to access your e-mail while traveling, be sure to ask before you assume you know what you're getting. And take plenty of different connection cords even if you are set up for wireless.

W.G. Williams
8/8/2005

The World's Best Fairy Tale...

Once upon a time, a guy asked a girl, "Will you marry me?"
The girl said, "NO!"
The guy then lived happily ever after and rode motorcycles and went fishing and hunting and played golf a lot and drank beer and scotch and left the toilet seat up whenever he wanted.

The End

Contributed by Gary Thornton
1/15/2009

You Can Always Ask a Gunny...

A young Marine officer was in a serious car accident and both of his ears were amputated. Since he wasn't physically impaired, he remained on active duty and eventually attained the rank of General. He was, however, very sensitive about his appearance.

One day the General was interviewing three Marines to be his personal aid. The first was an aviator and was a great interview. At the end of the interview the General ask him. "Do you notice anything different about me?"

The young officer answered, "Why yes, sir, I couldn't help but notice that you have no ears."

The general was not pleased with this lack of tact and dismissed him.

The second interview was with a female 2nd Lt., and she was even better. The General asked her the same question.

She replied. "Well sir, you have no ears."

The General dismissed her as well.

The third interview was with a Marine Gunnery Sergeant. He was articulate, looked extremely sharp and seemed to know more than the two officers combined. The General wanted this guy and went ahead with the same question, "Do you notice anything different about me?"

To his surprise, the Gunny answered, "Yes, sir, you are wearing contacts."

The General was very impressed and thought, "What an incredibly observant guy, and he didn't mention my ears."

"And how do you know I wear contacts?" the General asked.

The sharp-witted Gunny replied, "Well sir, it's pretty hard to wear glasses with no freaking ears to hold them up."

Contributed by Bubba & Bonnie Mehling
11/16/2007

You Gotta Love a Good Nurse!

A policeman was rushed to the hospital with an inflamed appendix.

The doctors operated and advised him that all was well, however, the patrolman kept feeling something pulling at the hairs in his crotch.

Worried that it might be a second surgery, and the doctors hadn't told him about it, he finally got enough energy to pull his hospital gown up enough so he could look at what was making him so uncomfortable.

Taped firmly across his pubic hair and private parts were three wide strips of adhesive tape, the kind that doesn't come off easily -- if at all.

Written on the tape in large black letters was the sentence, «Get well soon, from the nurse in the Ford Explorer you pulled over last week.»

Kind of brings tears to your eyes, doesn't it?

Contributed by Ron Heisler
11/8/2014

You Might be from Ohio if...

* You think all Pro football teams are supposed to wear orange!
* You know all the four seasons: winter, still winter, almost winter, and construction.
* You live less than 30 miles from some college or university.
* You know what a buckeye really is, and have a recipe for candied ones.
* "Toward the lake" means "north" and "toward the river" means "south."
* You know if other Ohioans are from southern or northern Ohio as soon as they open their mouths.
* You can spell words like Cuyahoga, Olentangy, Bellefontaine, Tuscarawas, Wapakoneta and you know which letter is doubled in Cincinnati!
* "Vacation!" means spending a day at Cedar Point in the summer and deer hunting in the fall.
* You measure distance in minutes.
* Your school classes were cancelled because of cold.
* Your school classes were cancelled because of heat.
* You've had to switch from "heat" to "A/C" in the same day.
* You know what should be knee-high by the Fourth of July.
* You end your sentences with an unnecessary preposition. For example: "Where's my coat at?"
* You install security lights on your house and garage and leave both unlocked.
* You think of the major four food groups as corn, pork, beer, and Jell-O salad with marshmallows.
* You carry jumper cables in your car.
* You know what 'pop' is.
* You design your kid's Halloween costume to fit over a snowsuit.

* Driving is better in the winter because the potholes are filled with snow.
* You think sexy lingerie is tube socks and a flannel nightgown.
* The local paper covers national and international headlines on one page but requires six pages for sports.
* You know which leaves make good toilet paper.

No trees were destroyed to post this message; however millions of electrons were terribly inconvenienced.

Contributed by Ron Heisler
10/27/2006

Your Tongue Can Be Your Worst Enemy!

Your words, your dreams, and your thoughts have power to create
conditions in your life. What you speak about, you can bring about.

-- If you keep saying you can't stand your job, you might lose your job.

-- If you keep saying you can't stand your
body, your body can become sick.

-- If you keep saying you're broke, guess what? You'll always be broke.

-- If you keep saying you can't trust a man or trust a woman,
you'll always find someone in your life to hurt and betray you.

-- If you keep saying you can't find a job, you will remain unemployed.

-- If you keep saying you can't find someone to love you or believe in you,
your very thoughts will attract more experiences to confirm your beliefs.

-- If you keep talking about a divorce or break up in a
relationship, then you might end up with it.

Turn your thoughts and conversations around to be more positive
and power packed with faith, hope, love, and action. Don't be
afraid to believe that you can have what you want and deserve.

Watch your Thoughts -- they become words.
Watch your Words -- they become actions
Watch your Actions -- they become habits.
Watch your Habits -- they become character.
Watch your Character -- it becomes your Destiny

The minute you settle for less than you deserve,
you get even less than you settle for!

Contributed by Susan Luna
7/12/2006

Contributors

Misty Ankney
Tom Benner
Renee Bernstein
Dennis Bialecki
Sharon Buckholtz
Tim Butler
Tod Butler
Chris Clody
Judy Flahiff
Ron Gargasz
Jamie Gillett
Julius Graw
E.W. Hallford
Ron Heisler
Mark Hopkins
Burt Kempner
David Lipschutz
Susan Luna

Bubba and Bonnie Mehling
Sherry Niese
Marshall Nestor
Eddie Kay Nichols
James Phillips
Eldon Reynolds
Kay Reynolds
Richard Sandford
Fred Schroeder
David A. Silverman
Barbara Stretavski
David A Taylor
Gary Thornton
James Tieper
Harvey West
Jaton West
W.G. Williams
Jeanne Zurat

In Memorium ...

Over the years, so many people have contributed to the content and success of the "Thought for the Day" that I can never adequately express my appreciation to each of them. Some of those contributors I've known since the late 1950s ... and some I've just met in the last year or two.

But looking over the pages of Volume One as I write this, many of those contributors have passed on and will be sorely missed. **Bill Derck**, a client and friend for a quarter century; **Chuck Furman** who worked with me and contributor Ron Gargasz at WBGU-TV in the late 1960's; **Jerry Johnson**, who welcomed me when I transferred to Lubbock High School in 1958; **E.W. Hallford, Michael Struve**, and **David Taylor** who were fraternity brothers in college; **Ron Heisler** and his wife **Dawn** who worked with me since 1995 here in Ohio; and **Bubba and Bonnie Mehling** who have contributed SO much over the years but who, I'm deeply sorry to say, I never actually met.

Unfortunately, there are many other contributors who I have never met as well. Many I've talked with on the phone and many more I've corresponded with ... and ALL are appreciated. Some of those folks may also have passed away since I've been unable to make recent contact.

And now the list continues to grow with this Volume. **Burt Kempner**, a very talented writer and friend with whom I've worked since the 1970's passed away as I was finishing this book; **Fred Schroeder**, another fraternity brother who will be sorely missed; and **Jeanne Zurat**, a lovely lady who I had only known for a few years passed away after making her first contribution to the Thoughts – and this book!

Without the contributions from each of them, these books would never have appeared.

About the Author

I've been sending out a "Thought for the Day" since the 1990s, and over the years it has become a meaningful connection with people from all walks of life and from many countries.

While I may be the one sharing these thoughts, I certainly cannot claim credit for them—many friends, readers, mentors, and inspirational voices have contributed these ideas, quotes, and reflections that helped shape these messages. I'm deeply grateful for the community that has grown around this tradition …and I'm always welcoming new folks who would like to join.

Sharing these daily thoughts has taught me the power of encouragement and the importance of pausing to reflect. My hope is that each "Thought" offers a moment of insight, kindness, or motivation to those who read it, just as editing them has done for me.

W.G. (Bill) Williams